My
Droid™

Craig James Johnston

que®

800 East 96th Street,
Indianapolis, Indiana 46240 USA

My Droid™

Copyright © 2011 by Pearson Education, Inc.

ISBN-13: 978-0-7897-4719-8
ISBN-10: 0-7897-4719-7

Library of Congress Cataloging-in-Publication Data is on file.

Printed in the United States on America

First Printing: November 2010

Trademarks

Warning and Disclaimer

Bulk Sales

Que Publishing offers excellent discounts on this book when ordered in quantity for bulk purchases or special sales. For more information, please contact

U.S. Corporate and Government Sales

1-800-382-3419

corpsales@pearsontechgroup.com

For sales outside of the U.S., please contact

International Sales

international@pearsoned.com

ASSOCIATE PUBLISHER
Greg Wiegand

ACQUISITIONS EDITOR
Michelle Newcomb

DEVELOPMENT EDITOR
The Wordsmithery LLC

MANAGING EDITOR
Kristy Hart

PROJECT EDITOR
Anne Goebel

COPY EDITOR
Geneil Breeze

SENIOR INDEXER
Cheryl Lenser

PROOFREADER
Apostrophe Editing Services

TECHNICAL EDITOR
Christian Kenyeres

PUBLISHING COORDINATOR
Cindy Teeters

BOOK DESIGNER
Anne Jones

COMPOSITION
Mary Sudul

Contents at a Glance

Table of Contents

About the Author

Craig James Johnston has been involved with technology since his high school days at Glenwood High in Durban, South Africa, when his school was given some Apple II Europluses. From that moment technology captivated him, and he has owned, supported, evangelized, and written about it.

Craig has been involved in designing and supporting large-scale enterprise networks with integrated email and directory services since 1989. Craig has held many different IT-related positions in his career ranging from sales support engineer to mobile engineer for a 40,000-Smartphone infrastructure at a large bank.

In addition to designing and supporting mobile computing environments, Craig writes about it for Smartphone Essentials and CrackBerry.com, a leading BlackBerry blog. Craig also cohosts the CrackBerry.com podcast and his own Mobile Computing Authority podcast. You can see Craig's previously published work in his books *Professional BlackBerry*, *My BlackBerry Curve*, *My Nexus One*, and *My Palm Pre*.

Craig also enjoys high-horsepower, high-speed vehicles and tries very hard to keep to the speed limits while driving them.

Originally from Durban, South Africa, Craig has lived in the United Kingdom, the San Francisco Bay Area, and New Jersey where he now lives with his wife, Karen, and a couple of cats.

Craig would love to hear from you. Feel free to contact Craig about your experiences with *My Droid* at http://www.CraigsBooks.info.

All comments, suggestions, and feedback are welcome, including positive and negative.

Dedication

To Dennis Ruyer on Dance Department and Derek "The Bandit" Richardson on Sound Republic for keeping my brain pumping at around 120 bpm while I wrote through the day and night.

Acknowledgments

I would like to express my deepest gratitude to the following people on the *My Droid* team who all worked extremely hard on this book.

A very special thanks to Justina Alicudo from Weber Shandwick for providing the Droids for screenshots and research.

Michelle Newcomb, my acquisitions editor who worked with me to give this project an edge, as well as technical editor Christian Keyneres, development editor Charlotte Kughen, copy editor Geneil Breeze, project editor Anne Goebel, indexer Cheryl Lenser, compositor Mary Sudul, and proofreader San Dee Phillips.

We Want to Hear from You!

As the reader of this book, *you* are our most important critic and commentator. We value your opinion and want to know what we're doing right, what we could do better, what areas you'd like to see us publish in, and any other words of wisdom you're willing to pass our way.

As an associate publisher for Que Publishing, I welcome your comments. You can email or write me directly to let me know what you did or didn't like about this book—as well as what we can do to make our books better.

Please note that I cannot help you with technical problems related to the topic of this book. We do have a User Services group, however, where I will forward specific technical questions related to the book.

When you write, please be sure to include this book's title and author as well as your name, email address, and phone number. I will carefully review your comments and share them with the author and editors who worked on the book.

Email: feedback@quepublishing.com

Mail: Greg Wiegand
Associate Publisher
Que Publishing
800 East 96th Street
Indianapolis, IN 46240 USA

Reader Services

Visit our website and register this book at quepublishing.com/register for convenient access to any updates, downloads, or errata that might be available for this book.

In the Prologue, you learn about the external features of the Droid and the basics of getting started with your Droid. Topics include the following:

→ Your Droid's external features
→ Fundamentals of Android
→ Installing synchronization software

Getting to Know Your Droid

Let's start by getting to know more about your Droid. We cover the external features, device features, and go over how the Android operating system works.

What Is Droid?

Droid is a clever marketing name given to Smartphones running Android on the Verizon CDMA cellular network in the United States. Android Smartphones that are given the Droid name can come from different manufacturers. For example, the original Droid comes from Motorola and its real name is the Motorola A855. The same Smartphone is available in GSM form outside the U.S. and is called the Motorola Milestone. Another example is the Droid Eris, which is actually made by HTC and is sold outside the U.S. as the HTC Hero. Now that you know what Droid is, let's take a look at the external features of the Droid.

Your Droid's External Features

The external features of the Droid vary slightly from one model to another. For example, some Droids have physical keyboards and a camera button and others do not.

Motorola Droid and Milestone

The Motorola Droid and Motorola Milestone are the same phone, so these external features apply to both models.

Proximity sensor   Earpiece   Light sensors   Power button   3.5mm headphone jack

Volume Up/Down button

Touchscreen

Camera button

Menu button   Home button

Back button   Search button

Microphone

Proximity sensor   Detects when you place your Droid against your ear to talk, which causes it to turn off the screen to prevent any buttons from being pushed inadvertently.

Light sensor   Adjusts the brightness of your Droid's screen based on the brightness of the ambient light.

Earpiece

Volume Up/Down button   Controls audio volume while playing music, watching a video, or talking on the phone.

Touchscreen   The Droid has a 480×854 pixel LCD (Liquid Crystal Display) screen with capacitive touch and a white back light. Because the screen uses capacitive touch, you do not need to press hard.

Microphone   Picks up your voice when you are on the phone.

Back button   Press to go back one screen when using an application or menu.

Menu button   Press to display a menu of choices. The menu differs based on what screen you are looking at and what application you are using.

Home button   Press to go to the Home screen. The application that you are using continues to run in the background.

Search button   Press to type or speak a search term. Your Droid searches your phone and the Internet for content that matches the search term.

5 Megapixel camera with autofocus

LED (Light Emitting Diode) camera flash

Back cover

Camera button

Speaker

5 Megapixel camera with autofocus   Takes clear pictures close-up or far away.

LED (Light Emitting Diode) camera flash   Helps to illuminate the surroundings when taking pictures in low light.

Speaker   Audio is produced when speakerphone is in use. Keep your Droid on a hard surface for the best audio reflection.

Back cover   Press firmly on the back cover to slide it downward when you need to swap the battery, Micro-SD card, or your SIM card.

Power button
3.5 mm headphone jack

Navigation pad

Physical keyboard

Power button   Press once to wake up your Droid. Press and hold for one second to reveal a menu of choices. The choices enable you to put your Droid into silent mode or airplane mode, or power it off completely.

3.5 mm headphone jack   Plug in your Droid or third-party headsets to enjoy music and talk on the phone.

Physical keyboard   Slide the keyboard out from under the screen to type.

Navigation pad   Move up, down, left, or right on the screen and press in the middle to select.

Motorola Droid 2 and Milestone 2

The Motorola Droid 2 and Motorola Milestone 2 are the same phone, so these external features apply to both models.

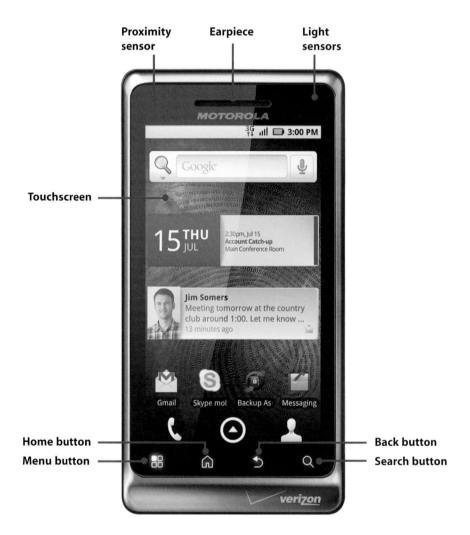

Proximity sensor · Earpiece · Light sensors · Touchscreen · Home button · Menu button · Back button · Search button

Proximity sensor   Detects when you place your Droid against your ear to talk, which causes it to turn off the screen to prevent any buttons from being pushed inadvertently.

Light sensor   Adjusts the brightness of your Droid's screen based on the brightness of the ambient light.

Earpiece

Volume Up/Down button   Controls audio volume while playing music, watching a video, or talking on the phone.

Touchscreen   The Droid 2 has a 480×854 pixel LCD (Liquid Crystal Display) screen with capacitive touch and a white backlight. Because the screen uses capacitive touch, you do not need to press hard.

Back button   Press to go back one screen when using an application or menu.

Menu button   Press to display a menu of choices. The menu differs based on what screen you are looking at and what application you are using.

Home button   Press to go to the Home screen. The application that you are using continues to run in the background.

Search button   Press to type or speak a search term. Your Droid searches your phone and the Internet for content that matches the search term.

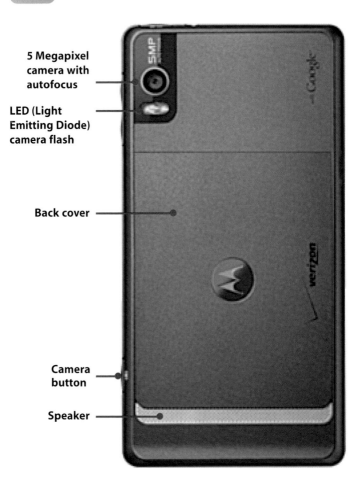

5 Megapixel camera with autofocus

LED (Light Emitting Diode) camera flash

Back cover

Camera button

Speaker

5 Megapixel camera with autofocus   Takes clear pictures close-up or far away.

LED (Light Emitting Diode) camera flash   Helps to illuminate the surroundings when taking pictures in low light.

Speaker   Audio is produced when speakerphone is in use. Keep your Droid on a hard surface for the best audio reflection.

Back cover   Press firmly on the back cover to slide it downward when you need to swap the battery, Micro-SD card, or your SIM card.

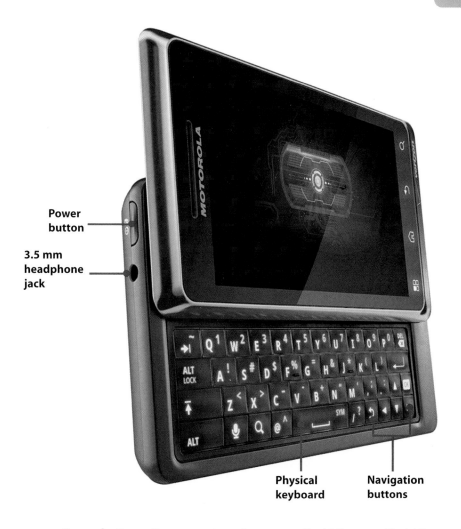

Power button   Press once to wake up your Droid. Press and hold for one second to reveal a menu of choices. The choices enable you to put your Droid into silent mode or airplane mode, or power it off completely.

3.5 mm headphone jack   Plug in your Droid or third-party headsets to enjoy music and talk on the phone.

Physical keyboard   Slide the keyboard out from under the screen to type.

Navigation buttons   Use the Navigation buttons to move up, down, left, or right on the screen.

Motorola Droid X

The Motorola Droid X does not seem to have a non-U.S. counterpart like the Droid, so this phone will likely be a Verizon U.S. exclusive.

Proximity sensor   Detects when you place your Droid against your ear to talk, which causes it to turn off the screen to prevent any buttons from being pushed inadvertently.

Light sensor   Adjusts the brightness of your Droid's screen based on the brightness of the ambient light.

Earpiece

Volume Up/Down button   Controls audio volume while playing music, watching a video, or talking on the phone.

Touchscreen   The Droid X has a 480×800 pixel AMOLED (Active Matrix Organic Light Emitting Diode) screen with capacitive touch, which does not require backlight. Consequently, it saves battery life and produces vivid colors. Because the screen uses capacitive touch, you do not need to press hard.

Microphone   Picks up your voice when you are on the phone.

Back button   Press to go back one screen when using an application or menu.

Menu button   Press to display a menu of choices. The menu differs based on what screen you are looking at and what application you are using.

Home button   Press to go to the Home screen. The application that you are using continues to run in the background.

Search button   Press to type or speak a search term. Your Droid searches your phone and the Internet for content that matches the search term.

8 Megapixel camera with autofocus Takes clear pictures close-up or far away.

LED (Light Emitting Diode) camera flash Helps to illuminate the surroundings when taking pictures in low light.

Speaker Audio is produced when speakerphone is in use. Keep your Droid on a hard surface for the best audio reflection.

Back cover Press firmly on the back cover to slide it downward when you need to swap the battery or Micro-SD card.

Video recording microphone   When recording videos, this microphone is used.

Noise cancellation microphone   While on a call, this microphone is used to determine background noise and eliminate it.

Power button   Press once to wake up your Droid. Press and hold for one second to reveal a menu of choices. The choices enable you to put your Droid into silent mode or airplane mode, or power it off completely.

3.5 mm headphone jack   Plug in your Droid or third-party headsets to enjoy music and talk on the phone.

Camera button   Press to activate the camera.

Micro-USB port ●
HDMI port ●

Micro-USB port   Use the supplied Micro-USB cable to charge your Droid X, or connect it to a computer to synchronize multimedia and other content.

HDMI port   HDMI (High Definition Multimedia Interface) has become the standard for connecting high-definition equipment such as plasma TVs and Blu-Ray players. This HDMI port enables you to play movies on your HDTV.

HTC Droid Incredible

The HTC Droid Incredible does not seem to have a non-U.S. counterpart like the Droid, so this phone will likely be a Verizon U.S. exclusive.

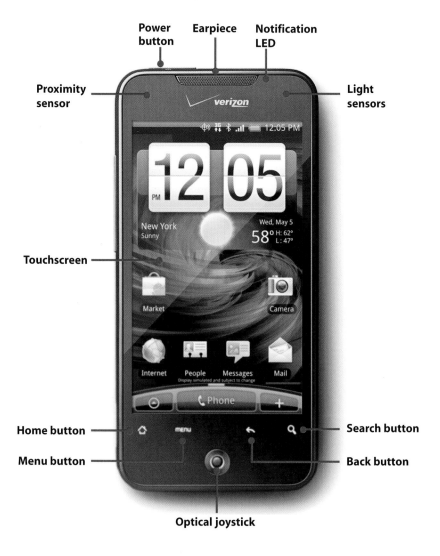

Proximity sensor   Detects when you place your Droid against your ear to talk, which causes it to turn off the screen to prevent any buttons from being pushed inadvertently.

Light sensor   Adjusts the brightness of your Droid's screen based on the brightness of the ambient light.

Notification LED   Shows solid green when connected to a charger or computer and is also fully charged. Flashes green when you have a pending notification (such as a new email). Shows solid red when the battery is being charged. Flashes red when the battery level is low.

Earpiece

Power button   Press once to wake up your Droid. Press and hold for one second to reveal a menu of choices. The choices allow you to put your Droid into silent mode or airplane mode, or power it off completely.

Touchscreen   The Droid Incredible has a 480×800 pixel AMOLED (Active Matrix Organic Light Emitting Diode) screen with capacitive touch, which does not require backlight and therefore saves on battery life and produces vivid colors. Because the screen uses capacitive touch, you do not need to press hard.

Microphone   Picks up your voice when you are on the phone.

Back button   Press to go back one screen when using an application or menu.

Menu button   Press to display a menu of choices. The menu differs based on what screen you are looking at and what application you are using.

Home button   Press to go to the Home screen. The application that you are using continues to run in the background.

Search button   Press to type or speak a search term. Your Droid searches your phone and the Internet for content that matches the search term.

Optical joystick   Navigate the screen or select items on the screen that are too small to touch with your finger. Slide your thumb over it and move it around to navigate. Press it to select items on the screen.

8 Megapixel camera with autofocus

Back cover

Speaker

Dual LED (Light Emitting Diode) camera flash

8 Megapixel camera with autofocus Takes clear pictures close-up or far away.

Dual LED (Light Emitting Diode) camera flash Helps to illuminate the surroundings when taking pictures in low light.

Speaker Audio is produced when speakerphone is in use. Keep your Droid on a hard surface for the best audio reflection.

Back cover Press firmly on the back cover to slide it downward when you need to swap the battery or Micro-SD card.

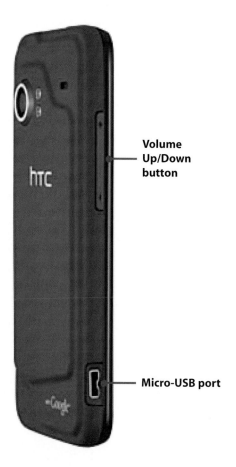

Volume Up/Down button

Micro-USB port

Micro-USB port   Use the supplied Micro-USB cable to charge your Droid Incredible or connect it to a computer to synchronize multimedia and other content.

Volume Up/Down button   Controls audio volume while playing music, watching a video, or talking on the phone.

HTC Droid Eris

The HTC Droid Eris does not seem to have a non-U.S. counterpart like the Droid, although many accept that the HTC Droid Eris is essentially an HTC Hero without the "chin."

Proximity sensor — Earpiece — Notification LED — Touchscreen — Home button — Menu button — Call button — Trackball — Search button — Back button — End/power button

Proximity sensor   Detects when you place your Droid against your ear to talk, which causes it to turn off the screen to prevent any buttons from being pushed inadvertently.

Notification LED   Shows solid green when connected to a charger or computer and is also fully charged. Flashes green when you have a pending notification (such as a new email). Shows solid red when the battery is being charged. Flashes red when the battery level is low.

Earpiece

Touchscreen   The Droid Eric has a 320×480 pixel LCD (Liquid Crystal Display) screen with capacitive touch and a white backlight. Because the screen uses capacitive touch, you do not need to press hard.

Back button   Press to go back one screen when using an application or menu.

Menu button   Press to display a menu of choices. The menu differs based on what screen you are looking at and what application you are using.

Home button   Press to go to the Home screen. The application that you are using continues to run in the background.

Search button   Press to type or speak a search term. Your Droid searches your phone and the Internet for content that matches the search term.

Call button   Press to answer calls, launch the phone, and place calls.

End/power button   Press to end calls. In standby mode, press once to wake up your Droid. Press and hold for one second to reveal a menu of choices. The choices enable you to put your Droid into silent mode or airplane mode, or power it off completely.

Trackball   Navigate the screen or select items on the screen that are too small to touch with your finger. Slide your thumb over the trackball and move it to navigate. Press it to select items on the screen.

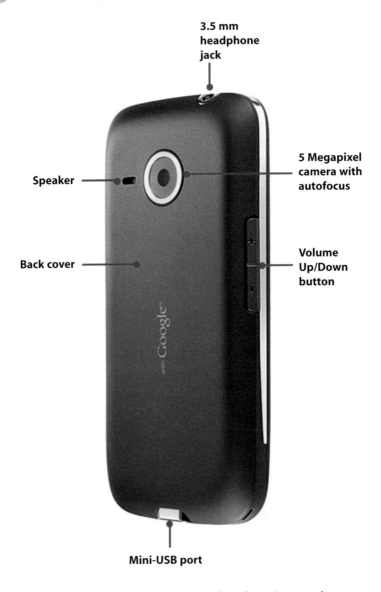

3.5 mm
headphone
jack

5 Megapixel
camera with
autofocus

Speaker

Volume
Up/Down
button

Back cover

Mini-USB port

5 Megapixel camera with autofocus   Takes clear pictures close-up or
far away.

Speaker   Audio is produced when speakerphone is in use. Keep your Droid
on a hard surface for the best audio reflection.

Back cover   Remove when you need to swap the battery or Micro-SD card.

Fundamentals of Android

Your Droid is run by an operating system called Android, which was created by Google to run on any Smartphone, and there are quite a few that run on Android today. Android works pretty much the same on all Smartphones with small differences based on the version of Android installed and the interface tweaks that each manufacturer may have made. Let's go over how to use Android.

The Unlock Screen

If you haven't used your Droid for a while, the screen goes blank to conserve battery power. To unlock your Droid, do the following:

1. Press the Power button.

2. Slide the green Padlock button to the right. This unlocks your Droid.

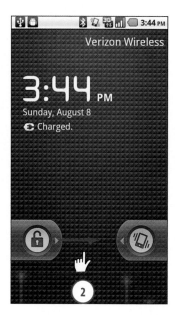

Silence Your Droid

On the unlock screen, there is a second button, which enables you to silence your Droid without having to first unlock it. Simply slide the yellow button to the left to toggle between silent mode and audio alert mode.

The Home Screen

After you unlock your Droid, you are presented with the Home screen.
The Home screen contains application icons, a Launcher icon, status bar,
and widgets.

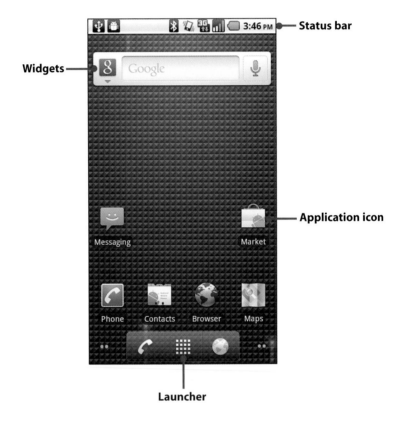

Widgets   Applications that run right on the Home screen. They are specially
designed to provide functionality and real-time information to the Home
screen. An example of a widget is one that shows the current weather or
provides a search capability.

Application icon   These are application icons that have been dragged to
the Home screen from the Launcher. When you touch one, it launches the
associated application.

Launcher   Touch to show application icons for all applications that you have
installed on your Droid.

Status bar   Shows the time, signal strength, battery level, and which type of network you are connected to, Wi-Fi or cellular. Also shows any notification icons such as new mail.

Drag the Status Bar

You can drag the status bar down to see more notifications or more details on the notifications. When the status bar has been pulled down, touch on a notification to be taken to the appropriate application.

HTC Sense UI

If you have a Droid Eris or Droid Incredible, you might be using the Sense UI from HTC. I do not cover all the Sense UI's functions in this book but refer to it every now and then. Although the standard method of seeing all your applications is to touch the Launcher icon, when you are using the Sense UI, you touch the up arrow to the left of the Phone icon to reveal your applications.

Your Droid's Home screen is actually composed of five parts or five screens. To see the other parts or screens, touch your finger on the right part of the screen and swipe to the left. You then see another part of the Home screen.

Many Droids do not come with any widgets or icons on these other parts of the Home screen, leaving them blank for you to populate.

>>> Go Further

WHAT ARE THOSE DOTS?

The small dots you see on the bottom left and right of the screen serve two purposes. They visually indicate how many screens there are to the left and right of where you are. For example, if you are on the main (or middle) screen, you see two dots on the bottom left, and two on the bottom right. If you swipe right, you see one dot on the bottom left and three on the bottom right, indicating that there is one screen to your left and three to your right.

If you touch and hold the dots, you see small thumbnail images of each screen. Touch the thumbnail of the screen you want to switch to.

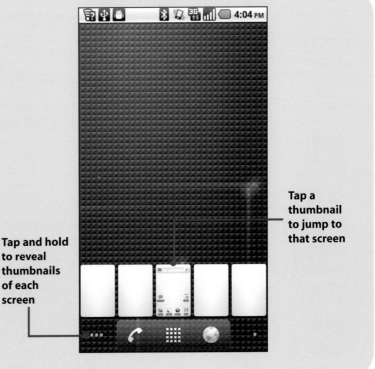

Tap and hold to reveal thumbnails of each screen

Tap a thumbnail to jump to that screen

Using Your Droid's Touchscreen

Interacting with your Droid is done mostly by touching the screen, what's known as making gestures on the screen. You can touch, swipe, pinch, double-tap, and type.

Touch To start an application, touch its icon. Touch a menu item to select it. Touch the letters of the onscreen keyboard to type.

Touch and hold Touch and hold to interact with an object. For example, if you touch and hold a blank area of the Home screen, a menu pops up. If you touch and hold an icon, you can reposition it with your finger.

Drag Dragging always starts with a touch and hold. For example, if you touch the status bar, you can drag it down to read all of the status messages.

Swipe or slide   Swipe or slide the screen to scroll quickly. To swipe or slide, move your finger across the screen quickly. Be careful not to touch and hold before your swipe or you will reposition something.

Double-tap   Double-tapping is like double-clicking a mouse on a desktop computer. Tap the screen twice in quick succession. You can double-tap a web page to zoom in to part of that page. Double-tap also works in the camera application. Double-tap to zoom the camera.

Pinch   To zoom in and out of images and pages, place your thumb and fore-finger on the screen. Pinch them together to zoom out or spread them apart to zoom in (unpinching). Applications like Browser, Gallery, and Maps currently support pinching.

Rotate the screen   If you rotate your Droid from an upright position to being on its left side, the screen switches from portrait view to landscape view. Most applications honor the screen orientation. The Home screen does not.

Your Droid's Secondary Navigation Method

Although you can do all things with your Droid by touching the screen, sometimes you might find it easier to use the included trackball, optical joy-stick, navigation pad, or navigation buttons to navigate and select icons, links on web pages, or small objects on the screen such as calendar entries.

To move around a screen or applications using the trackball or optical joy-stick, lightly touch the trackball or optical joystick with your thumb, and move it in all directions. The Motorola Droid has a directional navigation pad on the keyboard, and the Droid 2 has four directional buttons. As soon as your Droid detects that you are navigating with the alternative method, you see an orange block that highlights what you are currently hovering over.

The orange block shows which object you are hovering over

To select the icon or link on a web page that you are hovering over, press down on the trackball.

Using Your Droid's Keyboard

With the exception of the Motorola Droid and Droid 2, your Droid has a virtual or onscreen keyboard for those times when you need to enter text. You may be a little wary of a keyboard that has no physical keys, but you will be pleasantly surprised at how well it works. Let's go through the main points of the keyboard.

Some applications automatically show the keyboard when you need to enter text. If the keyboard does not appear, touch the area where you want to type and the keyboard slides up ready for use.

The Droid and Droid 2 both have physical keyboards that slide out from under the screen. As soon as you slide out the keyboard, the screen automatically turns to landscape mode. Although these Droids have physical keyboards, they both support the virtual keyboard in portrait and landscape modes.

Using the virtual keyboard as you type, your Droid makes word suggestions. Think of this as similar to the spell checker you would see in a word processor. Your Droid uses a dictionary of words to guess what you are typing. If the word you were going to type is highlighted in orange, touch space or period to select it. If you can see the word in the list but it is not highlighted in orange, touch the word to select it. This feature does not work when you are using the physical keyboard on the Droid or Droid 2.

To make the next letter you type a capital letter, touch the Shift key. To make all letters capitals (or CAPS), touch and hold or double-tap the Shift key to engage CAPS Lock. Touch Shift again to disengage CAPS Lock.

To backspace or delete what you have typed, touch the DEL key.

To type numbers or symbols on the virtual keyboard, touch the Symbols key. On the physical keyboard hold the ALT key while pressing space to see Symbols.

Touch space or period to select the highlighted word

Touch any other word to select it

Touch Shift to capitalize

Add Your Word

If you want to save a suggested word to your dictionary, touch and hold the word. You see a pop-up that shows the word and Saved next to it.

When on the Number and Symbols screen, touch the ALT key to see extra symbols. Touch the ABC key to return to the regular keyboard. From the extra symbols keyboard, touch ALT to return to the numeric keyboard or ABC to see the regular keyboard.

Quick Access to Symbols

If you want to type commonly used symbols, touch and hold the period key. A small window opens with those common symbols. Press the X to return to the regular keys.

To enter an accented character, touch and hold any vowel or C, N, or S keys. A small window opens enabling you to select an accented or alternative character. Touch the X to close the window.

Touch to type the character

Touch to close

Touch and hold to see accented or alternative characters

To reveal other alternative characters, touch any other letter, number, or symbol.

Touch any other letter or number to reveal alternative characters

Want a Larger Keyboard?

Turn your Droid sideways to switch to a landscape keyboard. The landscape keyboard has larger keys and is easier to type on.

Speak Instead of Typing

Your Droid can turn your voice into words. It uses Google's speech recognition service, which means that you must have a connection to the cellular network or a Wi-Fi network to use it.

1. While the onscreen keyboard is visible, touch the microphone key. Alternatively, you can swipe your finger across the keyboard from left to right. This does not work with the physical keyboard.

2. The microphone pops up. Wait for the message "Speak Now" and start speaking what you want to be typed. You can speak the punctuation by saying "comma," "question mark," "exclamation mark," or "exclamation point."

3. After you have spoken what you want to type, you briefly see "Working" and then your text is placed in the text field. The text remains underlined, so you can touch the DEL key to delete it. If you are satisfied with the text, continue typing on the keyboard or touch the Back button to close the keyboard.

Editing Text

After you enter text, you can edit it by cutting, copying, or pasting the text. Editing is done with the alternative navigation method (trackball, optical joystick, navigation pad) because it is easier to select text this way.

1. While you are typing, touch the text area.

2. Use the trackball, joystick, or navigation pad to scroll to the location where you want to cut, copy, or paste text.

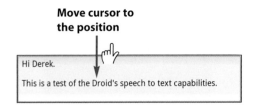

3. Press and hold the trackball, joystick, or navigation pad to reveal a menu. Choose the option that fits your needs. For the example, choose Select Text.

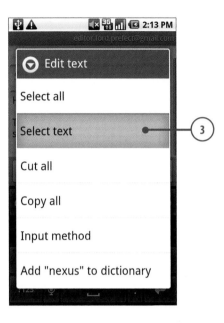

4. Use the trackball, joystick, or navigation pad to scroll over the text you want to cut or copy. Press the trackball, joystick, or navigation pad again.

5. Select either Cut or Copy from the menu and then use the trackball, joystick, or navigation pad to move the cursor to the location where you want to paste the text.

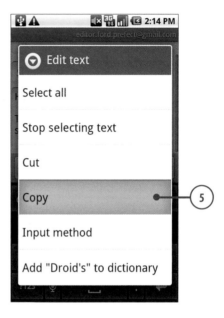

6. Press and hold the trackball, joystick, or navigation pad and select Paste from the menu.

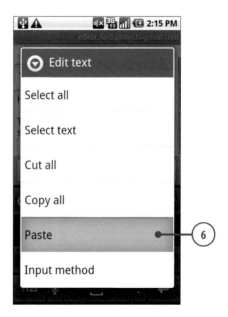

Starting and Switching Applications

We cover applications for your Droid in Chapter 10, "Working with Android Applications," but here is how to start an application and switch between them. Each application has an associated icon. Those icons can be on the Home screen or in the Launcher. The Launcher displays every application you have installed.

1. To start an application from the Home screen, touch the icon.

2. To open the Launcher, touch the Launcher icon.

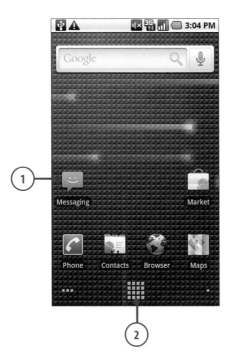

3. Because all the icons do not fit on one screen, the Launcher shows them falling off the bottom edge. Swipe upward to see more icons.

4. Touch the Home icon or the Home button to close the Launcher and return to the Home screen.

Switch Between Applications

You can quickly switch between recently used applications by touching and holding the Home button. A small window pops up revealing the most recently used applications. Touch an icon to switch to that application.

Menus

Your Droid has two types of menus: Options menus and Context menus. Let's go over what each one does.

Most applications have Options menus. These allow you to make changes or take actions within that application. Sometimes the Options menu has a More item that allows you to see more options.

**Touch the Menus
button to reveal the
Options Menus**

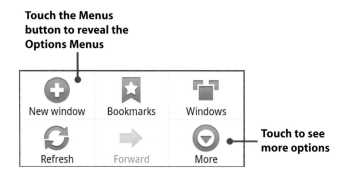

New window   Bookmarks   Windows

Refresh   Forward   More

**Touch to see
more options**

A Context menu applies to an item on the screen. If you touch and hold something on the screen (in this example, a link on a web page), a Context menu appears. The items on the Context menu differ based on the type of object you touched.

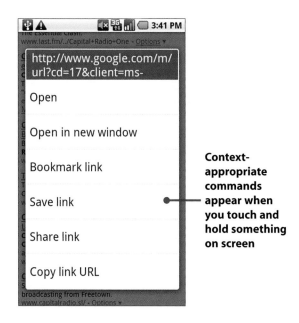

**Context-
appropriate
commands
appear when
you touch and
hold something
on screen**

Installing Synchronization Software

Your Droid is designed to work in a disconnected fashion without the need to connect it to your desktop computer. However you might still want to synchronize some content from your computer to your Droid. One of the most common uses for this software is to synchronize music and photos. In this book we use an application called doubleTwist. Other applications also provide synchronization for your Droid, such as Missing Sync from Mark/Space, but I've used doubleTwist because it is free. Before we begin, download the version you need (Windows or Mac OSX) from http://www.doubletwist.com.

Installing doubleTwist on Windows

1. Double-click on the doubleTwist install file. On the first screen, click Install.

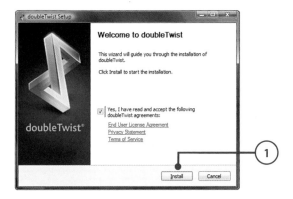

2. When the install is complete, make sure that the Launch doubleTwist box is checked.

3. Click Finish.

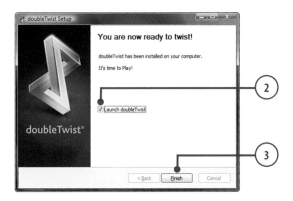

Installing doubleTwist on Mac OSX

1. Double-click on the doubleTwist disc on your Mac desktop.

2. Drag the doubleTwist icon to the Applications folder icon.

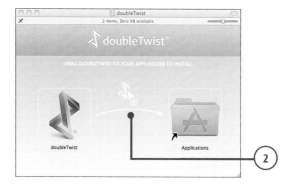

Creating a doubleTwist Account

The first time you run doubleTwist, it asks you to log in using your doubleTwist account. You probably don't have one, so let's go through how to create a free doubleTwist account. The steps and screens are the same for the Windows and Mac versions of doubleTwist.

1. Touch Create Account.

2. Type in your name, choose a password, and type in your email address.

3. Agree to the doubleTwist EULA.

4. Click Sign Up.

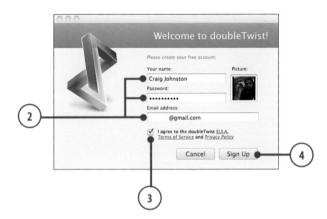

5. The next screen tells you to check your mailbox for an activation email. Switch to your email application and follow the instructions in the email. After your account is activated, switch back to this screen, and click Continue to start using doubleTwist.

In this chapter, you learn about your Droid's most important application, Contacts. You learn how to add contacts, synchronize contacts, join duplicate contacts together, and even how to add a contact to your Home screen. Topics include the following:

1

→ Importing contacts
→ Adding contacts
→ Synchronizing contacts
→ Creating favorite contacts

Contacts

On any Smartphone, including your Droid, the Contacts (People on HTC Droids) application is the most important. It is the central hub for many activities such as calling, sending texts (SMS), multimedia files (MMS), and email. You can also synchronize your contacts from many online sites such as Facebook and Gmail so as your friends change their Facebook profile pictures, their picture on your Droid changes, too. Let's open Contacts and look around.

Getting to Know the Contacts Application

The Contacts application runs on the Droid, Droid 2, and Droid X. Before we look around the Contacts application, let's open it. To do this, touch the Contacts icon on the Home screen.

Touch to launch Contacts

If you have never used the Contacts or People applications, you are prompted to add an account. If you have, you see a list of contacts. Before we jump into how to use Contacts and People, let's add at least one account. If you have already added one or more accounts, you can skip this section.

Adding Accounts

Your Droid can synchronize contact information with different online services including Facebook, Google (Gmail), and even your work Microsoft Exchange account. When you first set up your Droid, you would have already added a Google account (see Prologue) so we won't cover that type of account here. Let's go through how to add a Facebook and Microsoft Exchange account.

Adding a Facebook Account

If you have a Facebook account, you can synchronize your Facebook friends' contact information to your Droid. If they update their Facebook profile picture, their contact picture updates on your Droid. Here is how to add a Facebook account. Due to the differences in the Contacts and People applications, it is easier to add accounts through the Android Settings screens.

1. From the Home screen, touch the Menu button, and touch Settings.

2. Touch Accounts & Sync. On the Droid X, this menu item is labeled Accounts.

3. Touch Add Account.

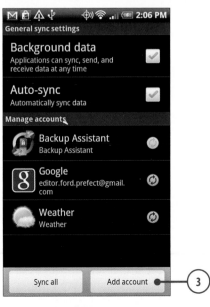

4. Touch Facebook. On the Droid Incredible and Droid Eris, you cannot touch Facebook, but you can touch Facebook for HTC Sense.

5. Enter the email address you used when you signed up for Facebook.

6. Enter your Facebook password.

7. Touch Sign In.

8. If you have a Droid or Droid 2, you must configure settings on an additional screen.

9. Touch Sync All to add all your Facebook friends' contact data to your Droid, no matter if you had a contact record for them.

10. Touch Sync with Existing Contacts to synchronize only contact data from your Facebook friends if they are already in your Droid's contact list.

11. Touch Don't Sync to not synchronize any contact data from Facebook.

12. Touch Next.

No Facebook Synchronization Choices

If you have a Droid X, Droid Incredible, or Droid Eris, you are not shown the previous screen. These Droid models default to synchronizing Facebook with existing contacts only as is noted in step 10. You are unable to change this.

Touch for Droid Incredible and Droid Eris

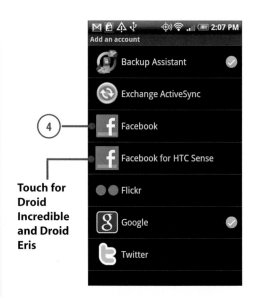

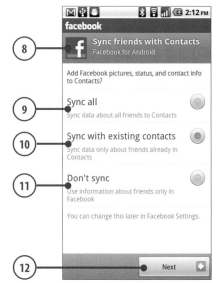

Adding a Microsoft Exchange Account

Your Droid can synchronize your contacts from your work email account as long as your company uses Microsoft Exchange. It might be useful to keep your work and personal contacts on one mobile device instead of carrying two phones around all day. Due to the differences in the Contacts and People applications, it is easier to add accounts through the Android Settings screens.

1. From the Home screen, touch the Menu button, and touch Settings.

2. Touch Accounts & Sync. On the Droid X, this menu item is labeled Accounts.

3. Touch Add Account.

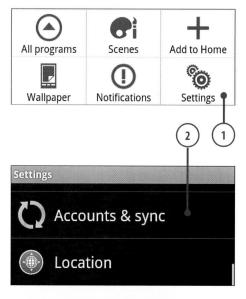

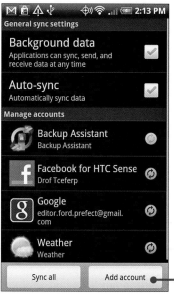

4. Touch Exchange ActiveSync. On some Droids, this might be called Microsoft Exchange ActiveSync. On the Droid X, it is called Corporate Sync, and on the Droid, it is called Corporate.

The Sequence Might Not Be the Same

Depending on the Droid you are using, the exact sequence of events and screen layout might not exactly match the following steps. However, you use the same information to add the ActiveSync account. On the original Droid, for example, you cannot skip step 5 by touching Manual Setup, so you have to enter your email address and password and then touch Next.

5. Touch Manual Setup.

Guess the Server

If you don't know what it is, you can try guessing it. If for example, your email address is dsimons@allhitradio.com, the ActiveSync server is most probably webmail.allhitradio.com. If this doesn't work, ask your email administrator.

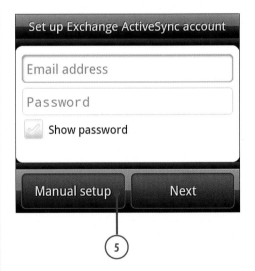

6. Enter your corporate email address.

7. Enter the name of your company's ActiveSync server.

8. Enter your domain name. This is the domain name you see every time you log in to your computer at the office.

Sometimes Domain Name and Username Are Combined

On some Droids, the domain name and username fields are combined into one field. In these situations, you must enter domain\username.

9. Enter your network username.

10. Enter your network password.

11. Make sure there is a check mark next to This Server Requires an Encrypted SSL Connection if your company uses a secure connection to its email servers. Most companies do use SSL.

12. Touch Next.

13. Select what you want to synchronize to your Droid, and touch Finish Setup.

14. On some Droids, you are presented with two extra screens before you complete the setup.

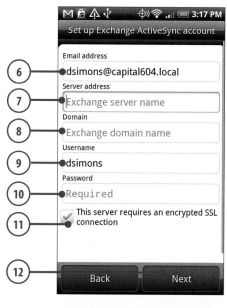

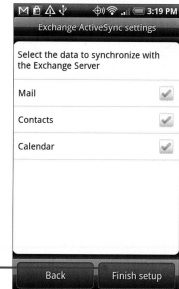

15. Set the Email Checking Frequency. This defaults to Automatic (Push). You can choose Push to have email delivered immediately to your Droid, choose polling intervals from 5 minutes to 1 hour, or set it to Never, which means only when you touch email will your Droid bring down the new emails.

Battery Life and Email Frequency

The battery life of your Droid is directly affected by how much work your Droid does during the day. The less time it spends checking for new email, the longer the battery will last. So with that in mind, if you really don't need to get your email in near real-time, set it to check once an hour, or only when you open email.

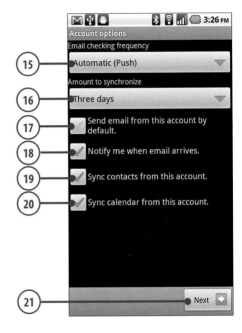

16. Set the Amount to Synchronize, which tells your Droid how far back in time it should keep your work emails. By default, it is set to One Day.

17. Touch to check the Send Email from This Account by Default option if you want to make your work email account the account used by default when you compose new email on your Droid.

18. Touch to check the Notify Me When Mail Arrives option if you want your Droid to notify you as new email arrives from work.

19. Touch to sync contacts from this account.

20. Touch to sync the calendar from this account.

21. Touch Next.

22. Give your work account a name.

23. Touch Done.

Remove an Account

To remove an account, from the main Contacts screen, touch the Menu button and touch Accounts. Touch the account you want to remove. At the bottom of the screen, touch Remove Account.

Display Options (Droid 1 and 2)

You can control how the Contacts application displays your contacts in two ways. You can set Contacts to hide contacts with no phone numbers, and you can choose which groups of contacts display for each account. Depending on the account type, the number of groups differs.

1. From the main Contacts screen, touch the Menu button and touch Display Options.

2. Touch Only Contacts with Phones to display only contacts that have phone numbers.

3. Touch the account to control which groups of contacts display.

4. Touch the check marks next to any contact groups you want displayed.

5. Touch Done.

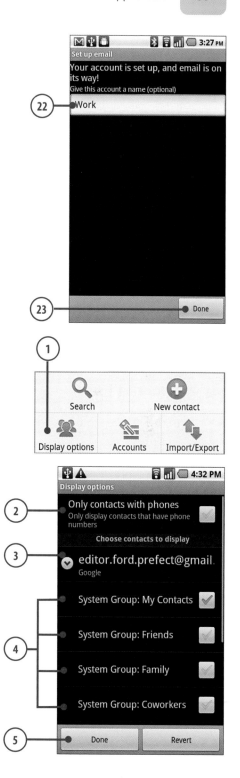

Display Options (Droid X)

On the Droid X, you have less flexibility than the original Droid when it comes to display options. You can filter the list of contacts by group or create a new group of contacts.

1. From the main Contacts screen, touch the Menu button and touch Display Group.

2. Touch a group to limit the display to just contacts in that group.

3. Touch Create New Group to create your own custom group and add contacts to it.

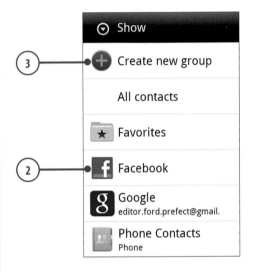

Display Options (Droid Incredible and Eris)

The Droid Incredible and Droid Eris use the People application for contacts.

1. From the main People screen, touch the Menu button and touch View.

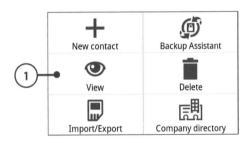

2. Touch to display only contacts that have a phone number.

3. Touch a group to show or hide them on the main People display.

4. Touch Done to return to the previous screen.

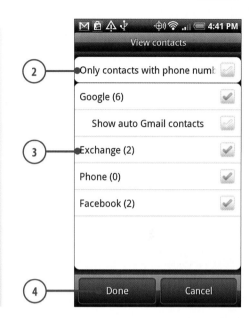

Adding and Managing Contacts

As you add contacts to your work email account or Google account, those contacts are synchronized to your Droid automatically. When you reply to or forward emails on your Droid to an email address that is not in your Contacts, that email address is automatically added to the contact list and duplicates are eliminated by merging information for the same name. You can also add contacts to your Droid directly.

Adding Contacts from an Email

Here is how to manually add a contact from an email. First you need to open the email client (either email or Gmail), and open an email. Please see Chapter 5, "Emailing," for more on how to work with email.

1. Touch the dot to the left of the person's name in the email. If your Droid is running Android 2.2, the dot is replaced by a blank contact picture.

2. Touch OK.

3. Touch the existing contact name you want to merge the new email address into.

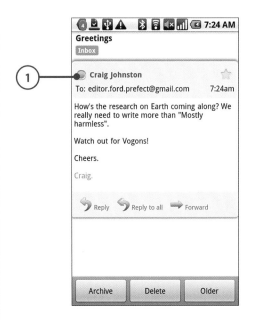

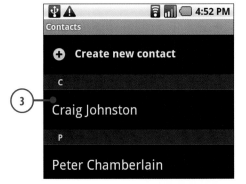

4. The new email address is merged into the existing contact. Touch Done.

Tap to change the label

New address added

Adding a Contact Manually

There are times when you meet someone and need to type his contact information into your Droid manually.

1. From the Contacts main screen, touch the Menu button and touch New Contact.

2. If you have a Droid 1 or 2, touch the account you want to add the contact to. Enter as much information about the new contact as you want.

3. Touch the down arrow next to Family Name to get more fields to fill out, such as middle name and phonetic given name.

4. If you touch the green + next to an item you can add multiples of that item, such as multiple phone numbers.

Choose an IM Account Type

When you add a new IM account, touch the label to the left of the entry field to change the type of IM to AIM, Windows Live, Yahoo, and many other types of IM accounts.

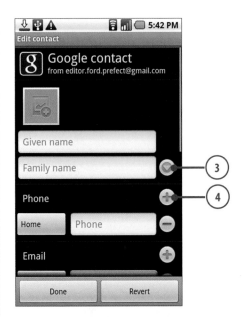

5. Scroll down to the bottom of the screen and touch More to add notes, nicknames, and websites for this contact.

6. Touch Done.

No vCard Attachment Support

Unlike other Smartphones, your Droid cannot deal with vCards attached to emails. Although you can import vCards if they are saved to your SD card, if they arrive as an email attachment, there is no way to import them. You need to import them using your desktop email client.

Joining and Separating Contacts

As contacts are added to your Droid, contacts are automatically merged if the new contact name matches a name that's already stored. Sometimes you need to manually join contacts together or separate them if your Droid has joined them in error.

Joining Contacts Manually (Droid 1 and 2)

Sometimes people don't enter their full names into their email clients and when they email you, their names might appear to not match existing contacts on your Droid. In this instance you need to manually join the contacts.

1. Open Contacts; then scroll to and touch the contact that you want to join a contact to. Touch the Menu button and touch Edit Contact.

2. Touch the Menu button and touch Join.

3. Your Droid guesses which contact you want to join to the first by listing choices at the top of the screen. Touch the name of the contact you are merging with.

4. The information from the contact you touched is merged or joined with the first contact. Touch Done.

④ — Done

Joining Contacts Manually (Droid X)

Sometimes people don't enter their full names into their email clients and when they email you, their names might appear to not match existing contacts on your Droid. In this instance you need to manually join or link the contacts.

1. Open Contacts, then scroll to and touch the contact that you want to link a contact to. Touch the Menu button and touch Link Contact.

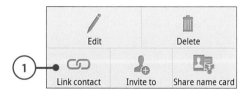

① — Link contact

2. Your Droid guesses which contact you want to link to the first by listing choices at the top of the screen. Touch the name of the contact you want to link with.

② — Craig Johnston

3. The information from the contact you touched is merged or linked with the first contact.

Joining Contacts Manually (Droid Incredible and Eris)

Sometimes people don't enter their full names into their email clients and when they email you, their names might appear to not match existing contacts on your Droid. In this instance, you need to manually join or link the contacts.

1. Open Contacts; then scroll to and touch the contact that you want to link a contact to. Touch the broken link symbol on the top right of the screen.

2. Touch All Contacts.

3. Touch a contact in the list that you want to link with.

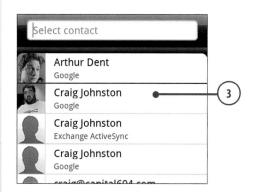

Suggested Linking

On the Droid Incredible and Eris, if you open a contact you might see that the People application has a suggestion about to whom that contact should link. On the top right of the screen, instead of the broken link symbol, you see the word Link with a number in green. That number represents the number of contacts that the Droid is suggesting you link with. If you touch the number you see a list of those contacts with broken link symbols next to each. Touch the symbols to select that contact to link with and then touch Done.

Separating Contacts (Droid 1 and 2)

Your Droid tries to join similar contacts together to avoid duplication. Sometimes you want someone to be listed more than once in your contacts, or you need to separate contacts that have been joined accidentally. Here is how.

1. Open Contacts. Scroll to and touch the contact that you want to separate. Touch the menu button and touch Edit Contact.

2. Touch the Menu button and touch Separate.

3. Touch OK to confirm the separation of contacts.

Separating Contacts (Droid X)

Your Droid tries to link similar contacts together to avoid duplication. Sometimes you want someone to be listed more than once in your contacts, or you need to separate contacts that have been linked accidentally. Here is how.

1. Open Contacts. Scroll to and touch the contact that you want to separate. Touch the menu button and touch Unlink Contact.

2. When asked if you want to separate two contacts, touch Yes.

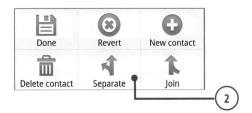

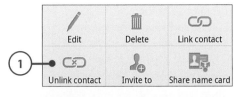

Separating Contacts (Droid Incredible and Eris)

Your Droid tries to link similar contacts together to avoid duplication. Sometimes you want someone to be listed more than once in your contacts, or you need to separate contacts that have been linked accidentally. Here is how.

1. Open Contacts; then scroll to and touch the contact that you want to separate. Touch the Linked symbol on the top right of the screen.

2. Touch one or more contacts you want to unlink.

3. Touch Done.

Organizing Your Contacts

When you have all your contacts on your Droid, you might need to organize them or share them with others. You can mark some contacts as favorites, move some contacts to your Home screen, and email your contacts' vCards.

Adding a Contact to Your Favorites (Droid 1 and 2 and Droid X)

You can mark contacts you communicate with frequently as favorites so that they are listed in the Favorites view on the main Contacts screen.

1. Open Contacts; scroll to and touch the contact that you want to mark as a favorite.

2. To mark a contact as a favorite, touch the star to the right of their name and the star lights. Touch the star again to remove the contact as a favorite.

3. To see only favorite contacts, touch the Favorites icon on the main Contacts screen.

Touch to see only favorite contacts

Droid X Favorites View

On the Droid X, to see only the favorites, touch the Menu button, touch Display group, and touch Favorites. The list of contacts lists only those people who are marked as favorites.

Adding a Contact to Your Favorites (Droid Incredible and Eris)

You can mark contacts you communicate with frequently as favorites so that they are listed in the Favorites view on the main People screen.

1. Open Contacts; then scroll to and touch the contact that you want to mark as a favorite.

2. Touch the Menu button and touch Edit.

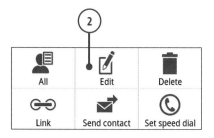

3. Touch the drop-down field under Group.

4. Touch Favorites.

5. Touch OK.

Adding a Contact to Your Home Screen

If you communicate with some contacts so much that you are constantly opening and closing the Contacts or People application, a quicker solution may be to add a shortcut to the contacts on the Home screen.

1. From the Home screen, touch the Menu button and touch Add.

Adding Shortcuts on HTC Droids Is Easier

On the HTC Droid Incredible and Eris that have the HTC Sense UI installed, you can touch the + button on the bottom right of the Home screen to add a shortcut.

2. Touch Shortcuts.

Touch to add a shortcut to the Home screen

3. Touch Contact.

4. Touch the contact. On the Droid Incredible and Eris touch Person.

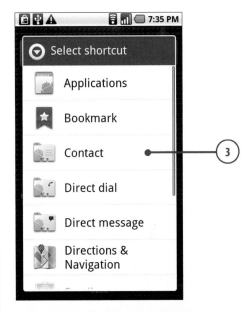

③

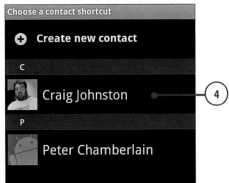

④

The contact added to the Home screen

Share a Contact
(Droid 1 and 2 and Droid X)

If someone asks you for your information or one of your contacts' information, instead of retyping it, why not send them a vCard right from your Droid?

1. Touch the contact you want to share, touch the Menu, and touch Share. On the Droid X, touch Share Name Card.

2. Choose either Gmail or Email. Email is your work email (if you set it up) and any non-Gmail accounts.

3. A new email opens with the contact information already attached as a vCard (.vcf).

4. Address the email.

5. Type a subject.

6. Enter text into the body of the email.

7. Touch Send. We cover email more in depth in Chapter 5.

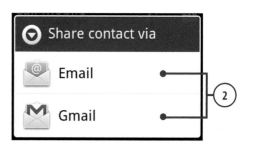

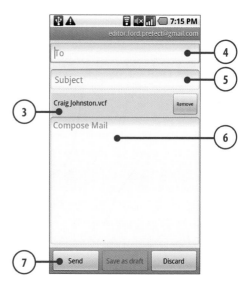

Share a Contact (Droid Incredible and Eris)

If someone asks you for your information or one of your contacts' information, instead of retyping it, why not send them a vCard right from your Droid?

1. Touch and hold the contact you want to share.

2. Touch Send Contact as vCard.

3. Touch fields to select and unselect them. This helps you exclude information from the vCard.

4. Touch to select how you want to send the vCard. Your choices are MMS, Mail, or Bluetooth.

5. Touch Send.

Communicating with Contacts

You can call your contacts, send them email, IM, text messages (SMS) or multi-media messages (MMS), and even write something on their Facebook walls.

Quick Contact (Original Droid only)

1. Touch the contact's picture to reveal the Quick Contact bar. The bar shows any status updates from Facebook or IM, and a row of icons that allow quick access to Facebook and Messaging (IM, SMS, and MMS).

2. Touch the Phone icon to see a list of phone numbers for the contact. Touch a number to dial.

3. Touch the Contacts icon to view the entire contact card.

4. Touch the Messaging icon to send the contact an SMS/text message, MMS, or IM.

5. Touch the Email icon to compose an email to the contact.

6. Touch the Facebook icon to view the contact's Facebook profile.

Status updates

Phone numbers

Messaging

Write on Facebook wall

Open contact

Email

Regular Contact

In addition to the Quick Contact method for communicating with your contacts, there is also the regular method.

1. Open Contacts and touch the contact you want to communicate with. Their full contact card appears with all information listed.

2. Touch to place a call to the contact.

3. Touch to send an SMS or MMS to the contact.

4. Touch to compose an email to the contact.

5. Touch to write on the contact's Facebook wall (original Droid only).

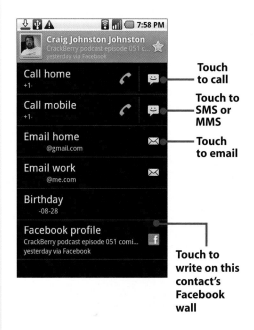

Touch to call

Touch to SMS or MMS

Touch to email

Touch to write on this contact's Facebook wall

Dial the Contact's Default Phone Number

Instead of first displaying all the contact's phone numbers, you can quickly dial the default number.

1. Touch and hold the contact's name. This reveals a new menu.

2. Touch Call Contact to dial the contact's default number. The line may read Call Mobile or Call Home depending on how the number is labeled.

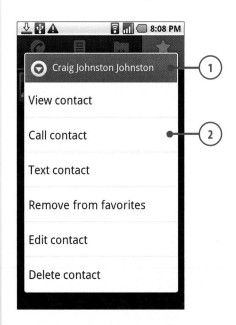

What Happens When They Call?

There are two additional settings for a contact that you may find useful. The first allows you to send a phone call from a particular contact straight to voicemail. The second is to change the ringtone that plays when a contact calls. To make these changes, touch a contact, touch the Menu button, and touch Options.

Importing and Exporting Contacts

Normally you allow your contacts to synchronize wirelessly over the air, but there may be a time where you want to import or export contacts with a desktop computer. This may provide you with a way to create a second backup.

Import Contacts from Your SIM Card (GSM Droids Only)

If you have just upgraded from a regular (or dumb) phone to your new Droid, you may have contacts stored on your SIM card. Here is how to import contacts from your SIM card to your Droid's Contacts application.

1. From the main Contacts screen, touch the Menu button and touch Import/Export.

2. Touch Import from SIM Card.

3. Touch the account you want to import the contacts to.

4. Your SIM card is read and after a few seconds, a list of the contacts is displayed. Touch each contact to import it.

5. Touch the Menu button and choose Import All to import all contacts found on the SIM card.

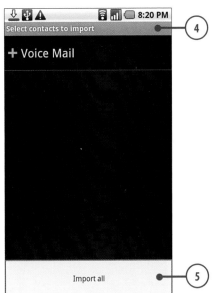

Import Contacts from Your Micro-SD Card

If you have some contact information saved on your desktop computer in the form of a vCard, you can copy those vCards from your computer to the Micro-SD card in your Droid and then import them to your Droid.

1. From the main Contacts screen, touch the Menu button and touch Import/Export.

2. Touch Import from SD Card.

3. Touch an option for importing one or more vCards.

4. Touch OK.

5. When importing only one vCard, touch the vCard that you want to import.

6. Touch OK.

Duplicate Names on a Mac

If you drag vCards from a Mac, you may see your vCard filenames duplicated with one of the file-names starting with "._". Ignore that file and use the one without the "._".

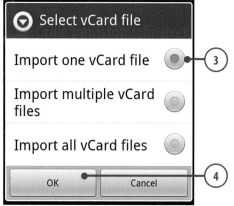

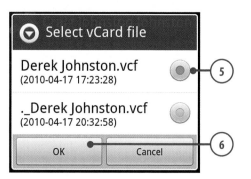

No vCard Picture

Even if the vCard you imported has a contact picture, your Droid does not display it. Hopefully, a future OS release will rectify this.

In this chapter, you learn about your Droid's Phone application. You learn how to place and receive calls, manage them, and use Google Voice as your voicemail. Topics include the following:

→ Placing and receiving calls
→ Managing in-progress calls
→ Setting up Google Voice
→ Using Google Voice for voicemail

Using the Phone and Google Voice

As with any good Smartphone, your Droid has a great phone that allows for making and receiving calls, voicemail, three-way calling, and many other features. However, your Droid can also use Google Voice to save you money on calls and to transcribe your voicemail if you want it to. We cover your Droid's phone in detail and go over how to set up and use Google Voice.

Getting to Know the Phone Application (Droid and Droid X)

1. Touch the Phone icon on the Home screen. The phone application launches and displays the familiar phone keypad.

2. Type a phone number.

3. Touch the green Phone icon to place the call.

4. Touch the Voicemail icon to listen to your voicemail.

5. Touch the Delete icon to correct a phone number, or touch and hold the icon to remove the entire number.

>>> Go Further

PAUSES AND WAITS

To add a two-second pause (symbolized by a ",") or a wait (symbolized by a ";") into your phone number, touch the Menu button, and touch the appropriate icon. When you touch Add Wait, your Droid dials the number up to the point of the wait and then waits until it hears a response from the other side. You can insert multiple two-second pauses if you need to. Pauses and waits can be useful when using calling cards or doing phone banking.

Touch to insert a two-second pause

Touch to insert a wait

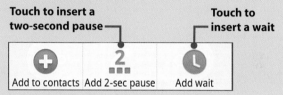

| Add to contacts | Add 2-sec pause | Add wait |

International Numbers

Normally when you dial international numbers, you have to use some kind of code before the country code. With your Droid, you don't need to know that special code; just type a plus sign, then the country code, and then the rest of the number, dropping any zeros before the area code.

Getting to Know the Phone Application (Droid Incredible and Eris)

1. Touch the Phone icon on the Home screen.

2. If you have a Droid Incredible, you see an extra window enabling you to choose to either launch the Phone or an extra application called AddressBook. Touch Phone.

3. Enter a phone number or a name using the letters on each number key.

4. Touch to delete a number.

5. Touch to hide the keypad.

6. Touch to display the People application. If you have a Droid Incredible, you once again need to select whether to see the standard Phone application or the extra AddressBook application.

7. Touch to dial the number.

8. Indicates the person is already in your contacts.

9. Touch to add the number to an existing contact, or create a new contact using the number.

10. Indicates an incoming call.

11. Indicates an outgoing call.

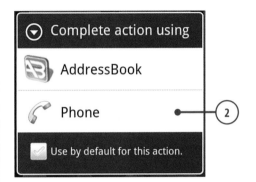

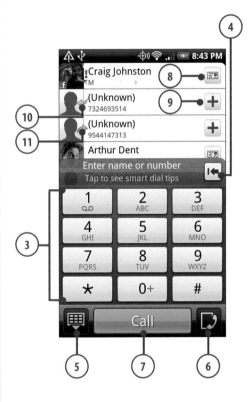

>> Go Further

PAUSES AND WAITS

To add a two-second pause (symbolized by a ",") or a wait (symbolized by a ";") into your phone number, touch and hold the Menu button, and touch the appropriate letter. When you add a wait (";"), your Droid dials the number up to the point of the wait and then waits until it hears a response from the other side. You can insert multiple two-second pauses if you need to. Pauses and waits can be useful when using calling cards or doing phone banking.

International Numbers

Normally when you dial international numbers, you have to use some kind of code before the country code. With your Droid, you don't need to know that special code; just type a plus sign, then the country code, and then the rest of the number, dropping any zeros before the area code.

Receiving a Call (Droid and Droid X)

When you receive a call, you have two choices for handling it.

1. Slide the green Phone icon to the right to answer the call.

2. Slide the red Phone icon to the left to send the call to voicemail.

3. If you miss a call, the Missed Call icon displays in the status bar.

4. Pull down the status bar to see how many calls you've missed.

5. Touch the Missed Calls notification to open your Droid's Call Log.

6. The Call Log shows all call activity including placed calls, incoming calls, and missed calls. Touch the green Phone icon to the right of a log entry to call the person back.

7. Touch a Call Log entry to see other actions to take for the call.

8. Touch Call <Name> to call the person back.

9. Touch Send Text Message to send a text message (SMS) to the caller.

10. Touch View Contact to see the caller's contact card if the person is already in your Contacts.

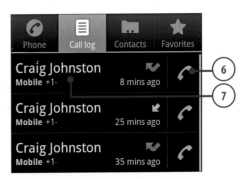

Clear the Call Log

To clear the Call Log, touch the Menu button and touch Clear Call Log. To clear just one entry from the Call Log, touch and hold that entry and choose Remove from Call Log.

Receiving a Call (Droid Incredible and Eris)

When you receive a call, you have two choices for handling it.

1. Slide the gray bar down to answer the call.

2. Slide the gray bar up to send the call to voicemail.

3. If you miss a call, the Missed Call icon displays in the status bar.

4. Pull down the status bar to see how many calls you've missed.

5. Touch the Missed Calls notification to open your Droid's Call History.

6. The Call History shows all call activity including placed calls, incoming calls, and missed calls.

7. Touch a Call History entry to return the call.

Clear the Call Log

To clear the Call History, touch the Menu button and touch Delete All. To clear just one entry from the Call History, touch and hold that entry and choose Delete from Call History.

Placing a Call (Droid and Droid X)

You can place calls on your Droid in a few ways including manually dialing a number into the Phone application, touching a phone number in a contact entry, commanding your Droid using your voice, and touching a phone number on a web page, in an email, or in a calendar appointment.

Dialing from a Contact Entry

1. Touch the Contacts application on the Home screen.

2. Touch the name of the person you want to call.

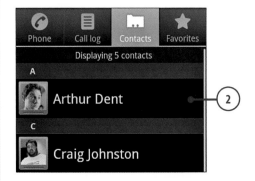

3. Touch the phone number you want to call.

Dialing from a Contact Entry (Alternative Method)

1. Touch the Contacts application on the Home screen.

2. Touch and hold the name of the person you want to call.

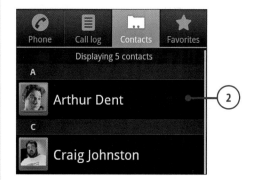

3. Touch Call Contact.

4. Touch the number you want to call.

5. Touch the Remember This Choice check box so your Droid remembers which number to dial when you call this contact.

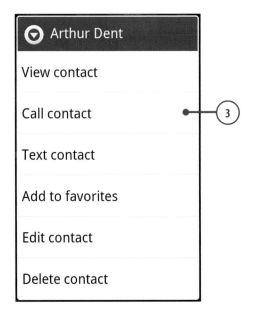

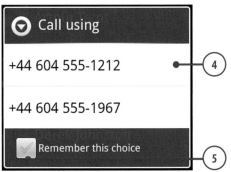

Dialing Using Quick Contact

1. Touch the Contacts application on the Home screen.

2. Touch the contact picture of the person you want to call (even if that picture is blank).

3. Touch the Phone icon.

4. Touch the number you want to call.

5. Touch the Remember This Choice check box so your Droid remembers which number to dial when you call this contact.

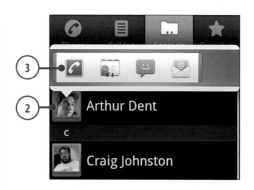

Set a Default Number

To set a default number for a contact, open the contact entry. Touch and hold the phone number you want to set as the default, and touch Make Default Number.

Dialing Using Your Voice

1. Touch and hold the Search button until the Speak Now box appears.

2. Say "Call" and the person's name. For example "Call Arthur Dent." Your Droid finds that person in your Contacts and displays the phone numbers on the screen.

3. Touch the phone number you'd like to call.

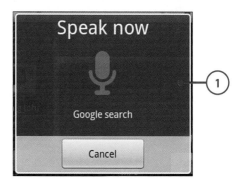

Be More Specific

If you know there are multiple phone numbers for a particular contact you want to call, you can be more specific when speaking your command. For example you can say "Call Arthur Dent Mobile" to dial Arthur Dent's mobile number immediately. This reduces the steps needed to place the call.

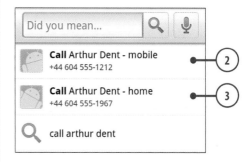

It's Not All Good

NO BLUETOOTH SUPPORT FOR VOICE DIALING

Voice dialing is a great feature, but as of the writing of this book, your Droid does not support voice dialing from your Bluetooth headset. While you are driving, this kind of support would make placing calls much safer. Let's hope this feature is added to future versions of Android.

Options While on a Call

While on a phone call, you can mute and unmute the call, switch the audio between your Droid and a Bluetooth headset, bring up the dial pad, and enable the speaker phone.

1. Touch the Pause icon to put a call on hold. The Pause icon changes to a Play icon. Touch the Play icon to take the call off hold.

2. Touch the Dialpad icon to display the dialpad and type additional numbers during the call, for example for phone banking. While the dialpad is displayed, the Dialpad icon changes to the Hide Dialpad icon. Touch it to hide the dialpad.

3. Touch the Bluetooth icon to switch the call from your Droid to a Bluetooth headset. The background of the screen turns blue when your call is directed to a Bluetooth headset.

4. Touch the Mute icon to mute the call.

5. Touch the Speaker icon to enable your Droid's speaker phone.

6. Touch the End icon to end the call.

Need to Know More About Bluetooth

Read Chapter 4, "Connecting to Bluetooth, Wi-Fi, and VPNs," for help on setting up Bluetooth headsets.

Conference Calling

While on a call, you can create an impromptu conference call by adding callers.

1. Touch the Add Call icon.

2. A second dialpad appears. Either type in the number for the person to call, or touch the Contacts icon to dial from your contacts.

3. Both calls display on the screen. The second call is in the foreground. If you touch the End icon, you hang up only on the second call.

4. Touch the Swap icon to switch between the calls.

5. Touch the Merge Calls icon to join the two calls together into one conference call.

Adding Multiple Callers

While on the conference call, touch the Add Call icon again to add another caller. The number of callers you can add to a conference call depends on what your wireless carrier supports.

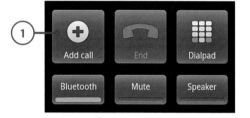

6. Touch the Manage icon to manage the conference call.

7. You see all of the callers on your conference call. Touch the red Phone icon to hang up on a caller.

8. Touch the green Split icon to remove the caller from the conference call and onto their own line.

9. Touch Back to Call to return to the previous screen.

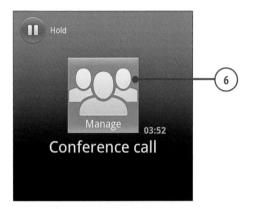

Placing a Call (Droid Incredible and Eris)

You can place calls on your Droid in a few ways including manually dialing a number into the Phone application, touching a phone number in a contact entry, commanding your Droid using your voice, and touching a phone number on a web page, in an email, or in a calendar appointment.

Dialing from a Contact Entry

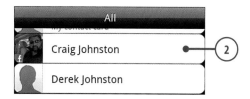

1. Touch the People application on the Home screen.

2. Touch the name of the person you want to call.

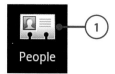

3. Touch the phone number you want to call.

DIAL A CONTACT QUICKLY

An alternative method of dialing a contact from the People application is to touch and hold on the contact's name and then choose which number you want to call.

>>> Go Further

Dialing Using Your Voice

1. Touch and hold the Search button until the Speak Now box appears.

2. Say "Call" and the person's name. For example "Call Arthur Dent." Your Droid finds that person in your Contacts and displays the phone numbers on the screen.

3. Touch the phone number you'd like to call.

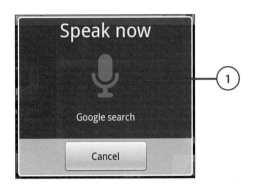

Be More Specific

If you know there are multiple phone numbers for a particular contact you want to call, you can be more specific when speaking your command. For example you can say, "Call Arthur Dent Mobile," to list Arthur Dent's mobile number at the top of the list. This reduces the steps needed to place the call.

No Bluetooth Support for Voice Dialing

Voice dialing is a great feature, but as of the writing of this book, your Droid does not support voice dialing from your Bluetooth headset. While you are driving, this kind of support would make placing calls much safer. Let's hope this feature is added to future versions of Android.

Options While on a Call

While on a phone call, you can mute and unmute the call, switch the audio between your Droid and a Bluetooth headset, bring up the dial pad, and enable the speaker phone.

1. Touch to end the call.

2. Touch to mute your microphone.

3. Touch to enable the speaker-phone. Touch again to disable it.

Need to Know More About Bluetooth?
Read Chapter 4 for help on setting up Bluetooth headsets.

4. Touch to view the contact information for the person you called, or who called you, as long as it is already stored in the People application. If the person is not listed in your contacts you are able to add him.

5. Touch to show the dialpad. This is useful if you need to use phone menus while doing phone banking or dialing into conference calls.

6. Touch the Menu button to reveal more options.

7. Touch to add a person to the conversation. See more about conference calling in the next section.

8. Touch to show the People application.

9. Touch to perform a Flash. Like landline phones, this puts the call on hold and enables you to take a second incoming call.

10. Touch to switch the audio of the call from your Bluetooth headset to the main phone.

Where Does the Audio Go?

By default, if you are paired with your Bluetooth headset before you make or receive a call, the call audio uses the headset. If you turn your Bluetooth headset on after you are on the call, your Droid automatically switches the audio to it.

11. Indicates where the call audio is going. Blue means Bluetooth, green means your Droid.

Conference Calling

While on a call, you can create an impromptu conference call by adding callers.

1. Touch the Menu button and touch Add Call.

2. A second dialpad appears. Either type in the number for the person to call, or touch the Contacts icon to dial from your contacts.

3. Both calls display on the screen. The original call is on hold.

4. Touch to merge the calls together into a three-way conference call.

Configuring the Phone Application

You can control how the Phone application works in many ways including whether to display your Caller ID information, how to handle call forwarding and call waiting, and changing your voicemail settings.

Phone Sounds and Alerts (Android 2.2)

If your Droid is running Android 2.2 (FroYo), the Sound and Display settings are separated. At the time of writing, the Droid and Droid Incredible were running FroYo.

1. From the Home screen, touch the Menu button and touch Settings.

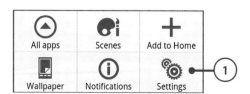

2. Touch Sound.

3. Touch to select the Sound profile. Sound profiles are only available on the Droid Incredible. This option on the other Droids is called Silent Mode and gives you the option to only enable or disable it.

4. Touch to adjust the ringtone volume. You can also adjust the media and alarm volumes.

5. Touch to select whether to vibrate when calls are received.

6. Touch to select the ringtone used for incoming calls.

Adding Custom Ringtones
See Chapter 3, "Audio and Video," for more information on how to add custom ringtones.

7. Touch to enable or disable the Quiet Ring on Pickup. This is only available on the Droid Incredible and silences the ringtone when it detects movement.

8. Scroll down for more options.

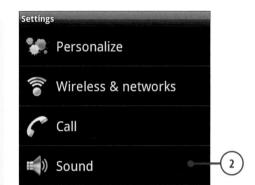

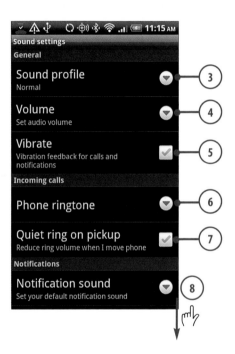

9. Touch to enable or disable playing tones when dialing numbers.
On the Droid Incredible, you can
also select whether the tones are
short or long.

10. Touch to select whether to enable
or disable an alert when you call
an emergency number such as
911. You can select a vibration or a
tone to play.

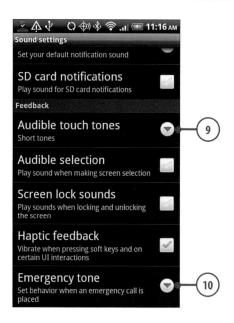

Phone Sounds and Alerts (Android 2.1)

If your Droid is running Android 2.1
(Eclair), the Sound and Display settings are combined. At the time of
writing, the Droid X and Droid Eris
were running Eclair.

1. From the Home screen, touch the
Menu button and touch Settings.

2. Touch Sound & Display.

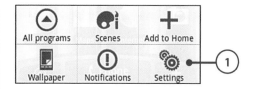

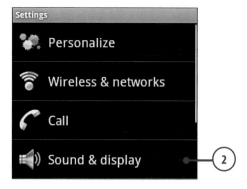

3. Touch to select the sound profile. Sound profiles are only available on the Droid Eris. This option on the other Droids is called Silent Mode and gives you the option to only enable or disable it.

4. Touch to adjust the ringtone volume. You can also adjust the media and alarm volumes.

5. Touch to select whether to vibrate when calls are received.

6. Touch to select the ringtone used for incoming calls.

Adding Custom Ringtones
See Chapter 3 for more information on how to add custom ringtones.

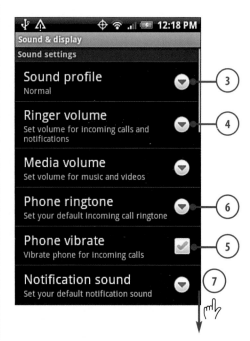

7. Scroll down for more options.

8. Touch to enable or disable Quiet Ring on Pickup. This is only available on the Droid Eris and silences the ringtone when it detects movement.

9. Touch to enable or disable playing tones when dialing numbers.

10. Touch to select whether to enable or disable an alert when you call an emergency number such as 911. You can select a vibration or a tone to play.

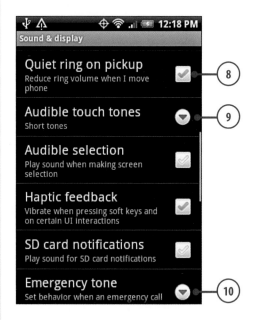

Call Settings

1. From the Home screen, touch the Menu button and touch Settings.

2. Touch Call. On the Droid and Droid X, this option is called Call Settings.

3. Touch to select your voicemail service provider. If you have Google Voice installed, you can select between Google Voice or your carrier.

4. Touch to change your voicemail settings. You might want to enter a new phone number for a different voicemail service instead of using your carriers.

5. Touch to clear the voicemail notification. This option is only available on the Droid Incredible and Eris.

6. Touch to enable or disable call automatic retry. When enabled, your Droid automatically tries dialing a number again if it fails to get through first time.

7. Touch to enable TTY Mode and select which mode you want to use. The Droid supports Full, HCO, and VCO.

8. Touch to enable or disable support for hearing aids, also known as HAC. If you don't use a hearing aid, make sure this option is disabled because it amplifies in-call volume.

9. Scroll down for more options.

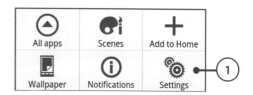

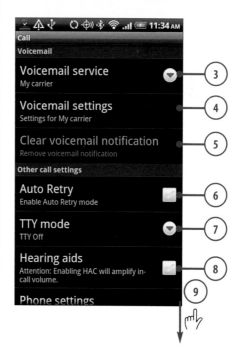

10. Touch to make a change to Phone Settings such as whether to prompt you to save unknown numbers to the People application when you end a call from an unknown person.

11. Touch to edit country code information. This option is only available on the Droid Incredible and Eris.

12. Touch to edit the Assisted Dialing Settings. These work in conjunction with the NBCD setting in step 11.

13. Touch to enable or disable an extra level of encryption on your voice calls. It has no effect on call quality.

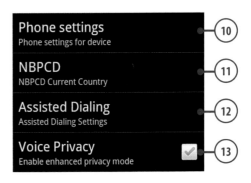

Google Voice

Regular Google Voice, if set up on your Droid, enables you to save money on international calls and have your voicemails transcribed into text. If you upgrade Google Voice, which is free, you have some extra features, such as choosing your own personalized phone number or setting up simultaneous ringing.

Setting Up Google Voice

If you want to start using the Google Voice features on your Droid, you need to go through some setup steps first.

1. Touch the Voice icon on the Home screen.

2. Read the welcome information from Google Voice and touch Next.

3. Select the account to use for Google Voice if you synchronize to multiple Google Accounts.

4. If you want to use a different Google Voice account, touch Use a Different Account to set it up.

5. Touch Sign In to proceed.

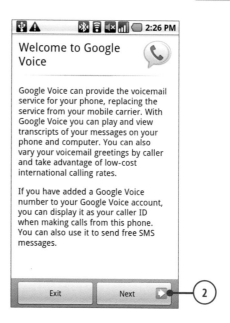

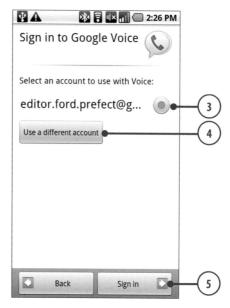

6. Touch Next to choose your Google Voice PIN.

7. Enter a PIN for your Google Voice voicemail box and touch Next.

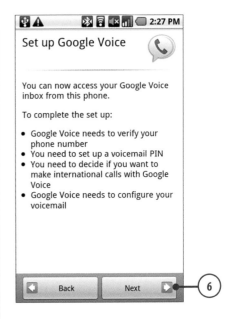

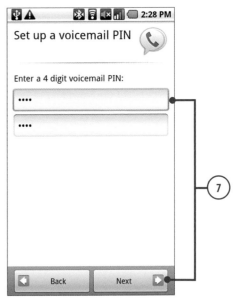

8. Touch an option for using Google Voice for international calls.

9. Touch Next.

10. On the next screen touch Next.

11. Touch Configure to continue to set up your voicemail to go to Google Voice or touch Skip to skip the step.

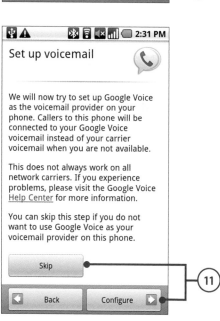

12. Touch an option to choose whether to leave the voicemail set to your wireless carrier or switch it to Google Voice.

13. If everything goes well, you see a dialog box confirming that your voicemail number has changed. Touch OK.

14. The Google Voice Inbox screen displays. Each time a call goes to your Google Voice voicemail, a new message appears in this Inbox. Touching the message reveals the transcribed text of the voicemail.

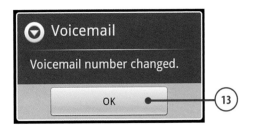

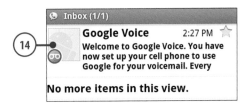

Upgrading Google Voice

If you want to use the advanced features of Google Voice, you need to upgrade your account. Upgrading is free of charge. To upgrade, use your desktop computer to go to http://google.com/voice.

1. Click Settings.

2. Click Get a Google Number.

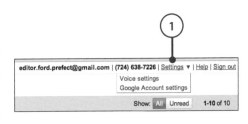

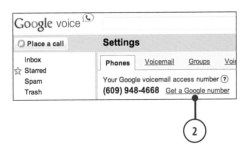

3. Click Continue.

4. Type search criteria in the box to search for available Google Voice phone numbers, including numbers that spell words.

5. Select a number from the options.

6. Click Continue.

7. Click Continue on the Confirm Your Number screen.

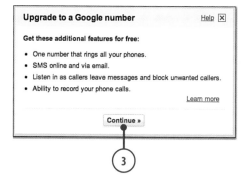

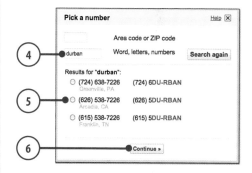

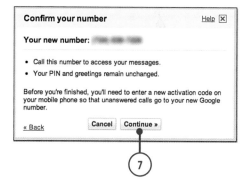

8. Enable call forwarding from your current mobile number to your new Google Voice number by following the instructions on the screen and touching Done.

It Might Cost You

Please be aware that some wireless carriers charge to forward calls, many times on a per forwarded call basis, so check with them before enabling the option to forward calls.

9. If the call forwarding has been successful, you see a confirmation. Touch OK.

Playing Back and Managing Voicemails

When you receive new voicemails, follow these steps to play them back and manage them.

1. Voicemails that you have received are displayed in your Inbox. To read and play back a voicemail, touch the voicemail.

2. Touch the Play icon to play the message audio.

Sometimes Google Guesses
Grayed-out words in a voicemail transcript are words that Google Voice is unsure of.

---

3. To take actions on the message, touch the Menu button. You can then call the person back, send a text message (SMS), view the person's contact information, add a star, and archive the message.

4. Touch More to refresh the message or delete it.

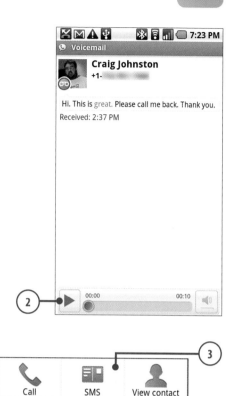

Send SMS and Check Your Balance

Google Voice allows you to send and receive text messages (SMS). You can use the main screen menu to do this plus check your Google Voice account balance, and filter the view by label. Touch the Menu button to reveal the menu.

1. Touch Compose to send an SMS.

2. Touch Balance to check your Google Voice account balance.

3. Touch Labels to filter the Inbox view by label. Labels include Voicemail, SMS, Recorded, and more.

4. Touch Help to load the Google Voice help web page.

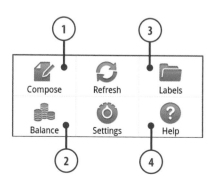

Google Voice Settings

After you have been using Google Voice for a while, you may want to change some of the settings.

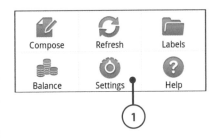

1. Touch the Menu button and touch Settings.

2. Touch Making Calls to change which calls go through Google Voice.

3. Touch Voicemail Playback to change where Google Voice voicemails are played.

4. Touch Refresh and Notification to change how often the Google Voice Inbox is refreshed on your Droid and to change the notification options.

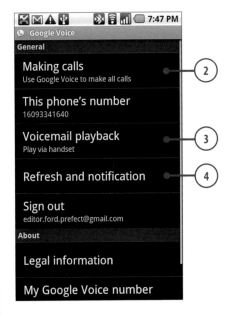

In this chapter, you'll learn about your Droid's audio and video capabilities, including how your Droid plays video and music, and how you can synchronize audio and video from your desktop computer. Topics include the following:

→ The Music application for audio and music

→ The Gallery application for video

→ YouTube

→ Using doubleTwist to synchronize audio and video

Audio and Video

Your Droid is a strong multimedia Smartphone with the ability play back many different audio and video formats. The large screen enables you to turn your Droid sideways to enjoy a video in its original 16:9 ratio. You can also use your Droid to search YouTube, watch videos, and even upload videos to YouTube right from your phone.

The Music Application—Audio (Droid and Droid X)

Let's take a look at how the Music application works and how to enjoy hours of music while you work.

1. Touch the Music icon on the Home screen. The Music application presents you with any music and audio files that you have copied to your Droid.

2. Touch Artists to filter the view by artist. Touch an artist's name to reveal songs by that artist and then touch a song to play it.

3. Touch Albums to filter the view by album title. Touch an album name to reveal songs on that album and then touch a song to play it.

4. Touch Songs to filter the view by song title. This shows all songs by all artists. Touch a song to play it.

5. Touch Playlists to show any music playlists that you have synchronized to your Droid. We cover how to do that later in the chapter.

Don't Forget the Search Button

One important thing to remember is the Search button. No matter what view you are in, you can always touch the Search button and either type or speak your search.

SCROLL BY LETTER

>>> Go Further

In any view you can scroll through your albums, artists, or songs quickly by touching the scroll box that pops out on the right of the screen. Move it up and down to jump to items beginning with the letter of the alphabet that shows in the large box. So for example, to jump to artists that begin with the letter D, scroll until you see the letter D appear in the large box, and then release the scroll box.

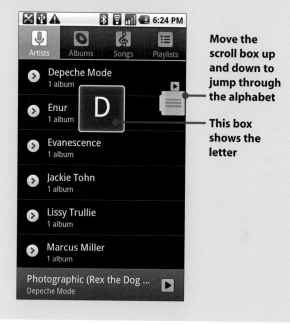

Move the scroll box up and down to jump through the alphabet

This box shows the letter

Controlling Playback

While your music is playing, you have some control over how it plays, and the selection of music that plays.

1. Touch to jump to the previous song in the album, playlist, or shuffle. Touch and hold to rewind the song.

2. Touch to jump to the next song in the album, playlist, or shuffle. Touch and hold to fast forward the song.

3. Touch to pause the song. The button turns into the Play button when a song is paused. Touch again to resume playing a paused song.

4. Touch to open the current playlist. If the song is not in a playlist, the list of all songs displays.

5. Touch to shuffle the current playlist. This plays the songs in the playlist in random order. If the song is not in a playlist, all songs on your Droid are be shuffled.

6. Touch to enable repeating. Touch once to repeat all songs, touch again to repeat the current song only, touch again to disable repeating.

7. Drag to skip through the song.

8. Press the volume control on the left of your Droid to increase or decrease the volume of the music. A Media Volume window pops up and displays the volume level visually.

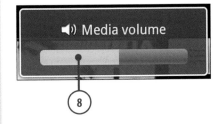

Taking More Actions

While a song is playing, if you touch the Menu button, you can take a few actions on the song.

1. Touch to see your entire music library.

2. Touch to add the current song to a playlist.

3. Touch to use the song as the current ringtone for your Droid.

4. Touch to delete the current song. Confirm the deletion on the next screen.

5. Touch to let your Droid start the Party Shuffle feature.

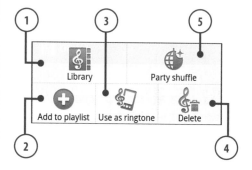

Your Droid Is the Party DJ

When you enable Party Shuffle, your Droid creates an on-the-fly playlist and chooses 12 random tracks for it. As it nears the end of the playlist, it adds another 12 random tracks. It keeps doing this until your turn off Party Shuffle.

Working and Listening to Music

While your music is playing, you can continue using your Droid without interrupting the music.

1. To work on other applications while listening to music, touch the Home button. The notification bar displays an icon indicating your music is still playing.

2. To switch back to the currently playing song, pull down the notification bar.

3. Touch the song.

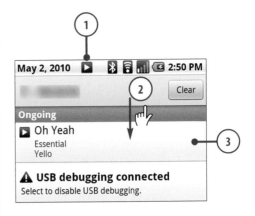

What If I Get a Call?

If someone calls you while you are listening to music, your Droid pauses the music and displays the regular incoming call screen. After you hang up, the music continues playing.

Managing Playlists (Droid and Droid X)

Playlists allow you to group songs together. Here is how to create them and use them.

Creating a New Playlist on Your Droid

To create a new playlist, you must already know the first song you want to add to it.

1. Touch and hold a song.

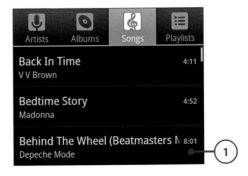

2. Touch Add to Playlist.

3. Touch New.

4. Type in the name of the playlist.

5. Touch Save.

Create a Playlist While Listening

You can create a playlist while listening to the song you want to use to create that playlist with. Touch the Menu button and choose Add to Playlist.

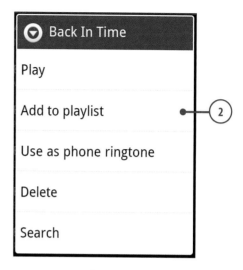

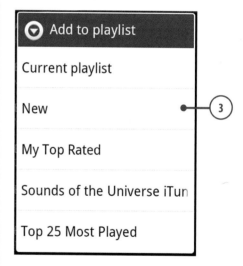

Adding a Song to an Existing Playlist

1. While listening to a song, touch the Menu button. Then touch Add to Playlist.

2. Touch the playlist you want to add the song to.

Add to Playlist from Library
You can also add a song to a playlist when viewing your song library. Touch and hold on a song; then choose Add to Playlist.

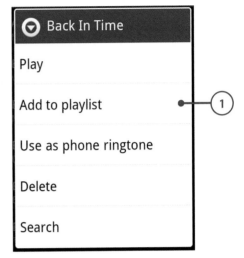

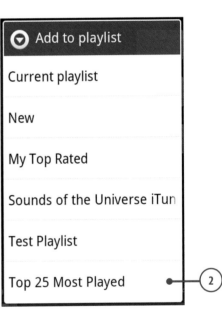

Rearranging Songs in a Playlist

1. Touch a Playlist to show the songs in it.

2. Touch and hold the three lines to the left of a song you want to move. Move that song up and down until it is in the right place, and then release it.

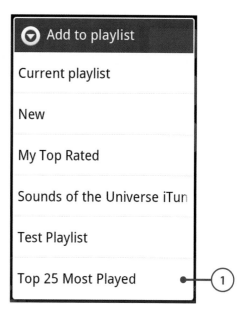

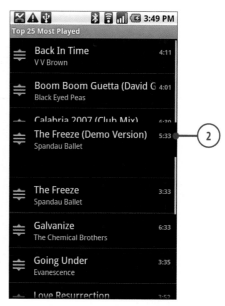

Clearing a Playlist

1. Touch a Playlist to show the songs in it.

2. Touch Menu and touch Clear Playlist. Be careful because there is no warning; the playlist is cleared immediately.

It's Not All Good

CLEARING BUGS

There seem to be some bugs with clearing playlists. First, the Clear Playlist menu item is not visible unless you are playing a song from that playlist. Second, when you touch Clear Playlist, it is not actually cleared. If you go back to the Playlist view and touch that playlist, all the songs are still listed. Hopefully this will be fixed in a new version of Android.

Deleting and Renaming a Playlist

1. Touch Playlists to show the list of playlists.

2. Touch and hold on the playlist you'd like to rename or delete.

3. Touch Delete to delete the playlist. Be careful because there is no warning; the playlist is immediately deleted.

4. Touch Rename to rename the playlist. Type in the new name and touch Save.

Songs Not Deleted

When you clear or delete a playlist, remember that the songs listed in them are not deleted from your Droid. Playlists are just groupings of song names.

Manually Creating a Playlist on a Computer

When we cover doubleTwist later in this chapter, we go over how to synchronize playlists from iTunes, but there is another way to create playlists. If you feel like having complete control over the creation process, these are the steps.

1. Gather the songs you want to place in your new playlist in their own folder on your computer.

2. Use a text editor to create a new text file. (Notepad in Windows or TextEdit on the Mac will do.) Type this text at the top of the file:

    #EXTM3U

3. Type the filenames for each song you want in the playlist, each on a separate line.

4. Save the text file and make sure the file extension is .m3u.

5. Connect your Droid to your computer using the USB cable. On your Droid, drag down the notification area.

6. Touch USB Connected.

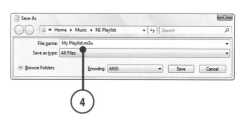

7. Touch Mount to mount your Droid as a new drive in Windows or OSX.

8. Drag your folder that contains the songs and the playlist file to your Droid. You can put it anywhere. Then, on your desktop computer, eject the Droid by right-clicking on it and selecting Eject.

9. On your Droid, drag down the notification area again, but this time touch Turn off USB storage. When your Droid finishes processing the new files, it plays a sound. Your new songs and playlist should be successfully loaded.

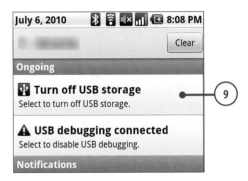

The Music Application—Audio (Droid Incredible and Eris)

Let's take a look at how the Music application works and how to enjoy hours of music while you work.

1. Touch the Music icon on the Home screen. The Music application presents you with any music and audio files that you have copied to your Droid.

2. Touch to enable or disable shuffle mode. This is where your Droid randomly selects tracks to play.

3. Touch to repeat all songs; touch again to repeat just the current song; touch again to disable.

4. Touch and scroll left and right to view all songs.

5. Touch to view the Now Playing songs in a list.

6. Touch to jump to the previous song.

7. Touch to pause the song. Touch again to resume playing.

8. Touch to jump to the next song.

9. Touch to see all of your music filtered by artist, album, playlist, genre, and composer.

Viewing Your Music

While your music is playing, you can scroll left and right through the tracks, or you can see all of your music filtered, which makes it easier to find what you are looking for.

1. Touch to view music filters.

2. Touch to view songs by album.

3. Touch to view playlists.

4. Touch to see all songs.

5. Touch to see songs grouped by genre.

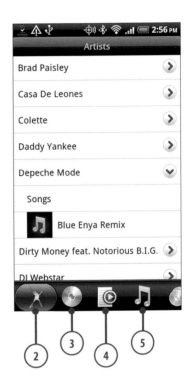

Taking More Actions

While a song is playing, if you touch the Menu button, you can take a few actions on the song.

1. Touch to share the song over Bluetooth. This actually sends the music file to another device over Bluetooth. This normally only works when sending to a computer, not to another phone.

2. Touch to add the current song to a playlist. You are presented with a list of playlists. Touch one, or add a new playlist.

3. Touch to use the song as the current ringtone for your Droid.

4. Touch to see more details about the song.

5. Touch to enable shuffle mode.

6. Touch to repeat the song.

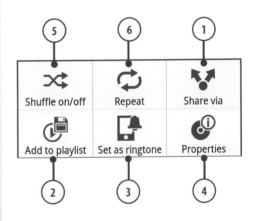

Working and Listening to Music

While your music is playing, you can continue using your Droid without interrupting the music.

1. To work on other applications while listening to music, touch the Home button. The notification bar displays an icon indicating your music is still playing.

2. To switch back to the currently playing song, pull down the notification bar.

3. Touch the song.

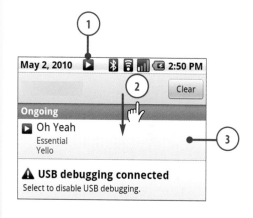

What If I Get a Call?

If someone calls you while you are listening to music, your Droid pauses the music and displays the regular incoming call screen. After you hang up, the music continues playing.

Managing Playlists (Droid Incredible and Eris)

Playlists allow you to group songs together. Here is how to create them and use them.

Creating a New Playlist on Your Droid

You can create a new playlist anytime. Here is how.

1. Touch to see the filtered song view.

2. Touch to see the Playlist view.

3. Type the name of the playlist.

4. Touch to add songs to the playlist.

5. Touch on an artist.

6. Touch to select one or more songs.

7. Touch to continue.

Select All or Nothing

While selecting songs to add to your playlist, if you touch the Menu button you can touch Select All or Unselect All.

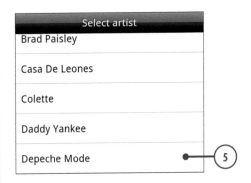

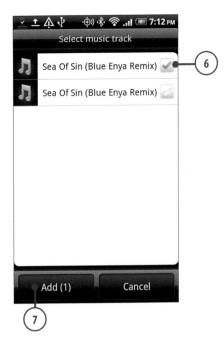

8. Touch to remove a song from the playlist.

9. Touch to save the playlist.

Adding a Song to an Existing Playlist

1. While listening to a song, touch the Menu button. Then touch Add to Playlist.

2. Touch the playlist you want to add the song to.

Add to Playlist from Library

You can also add a song to a playlist when viewing your song library. Touch and hold on a song; then choose Add to Playlist.

Rearranging Songs in a Playlist

1. Touch a Playlist to show the songs in it.

2. Touch the Menu button and touch Change Order.

3. Touch and hold the three lines to the left of a song you want to move. Move that song up and down until it is in the right place and then release it.

4. Touch Done to save your changes.

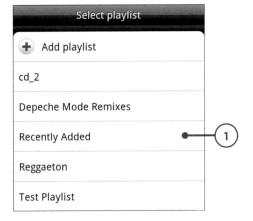

Renaming or Deleting a Playlist

To rename or delete a playlist, start by touching and holding the name of the playlist you want to change.

1. Touch to delete the playlist.

2. Touch to rename the playlist.

Songs Not Deleted

When you clear or delete a playlist, remember that the songs listed in them are not deleted from your Droid. Playlists are just groupings of song names.

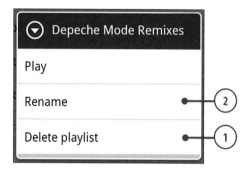

The Gallery Application—Video (Droid 1)

The Gallery application allows you to view pictures and video, and share pictures and video with people via MMS, Bluetooth, YouTube, and email. We cover viewing and sharing videos in this chapter and cover pictures in Chapter 9, "Taking, Storing, and Viewing Pictures."

1. Touch the Gallery icon to launch the Gallery application.

2. Albums that contain videos have a little Play icon. Touch an album to view available videos.

3. Touch a video to start playing it.

4. While a video is playing, touch the screen to reveal the playback controls.

5. Touch to jump backward a few seconds.

6. Touch to pause the video, and touch again to resume playing it.

7. Touch to jump forward a few seconds.

8. Drag left and right to move rapidly forward and backward through the video.

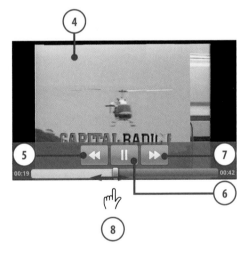

Sharing Videos

You can share small videos with people from the Gallery application. Here is how.

1. Touch the Menu button twice to show the Gallery Menu.

2. Touch one or more videos. Videos you've selected have a green check mark.

3. Touch Share.

4. Touch a method for sharing the videos.

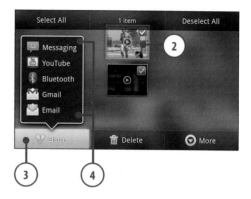

Small Video Size

You can only share very small videos from your Droid. The video file size cannot exceed 3Mb, which is about 1 minute of high-quality video, or about 2 minutes of low-quality video. This is true for all types of video sharing, excepting MMS, where the videos can only be 30 seconds long.

Sharing Video Using MMS

1. Address the MMS.

2. Type an optional message to go with the video.

3. Touch to send the MMS.

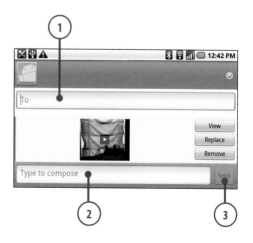

Sharing Video Using Bluetooth

1. Touch the previously paired Bluetooth device. If the paired device accepts Bluetooth file sharing, the video is sent. We cover how to pair Bluetooth devices in Chapter 4, "Connecting to Bluetooth, Wi-Fi, and VPNs."

Bluetooth Sharing Might Fail

Many phones do not accept incoming Bluetooth files, but devices like computers do. Even on computers, the recipient must configure her Bluetooth configuration to accept incoming files.

Sharing Video Using Email or Gmail

1. Address the email.

2. Type an optional subject.

3. Type an optional message.

4. Touch to send the email.

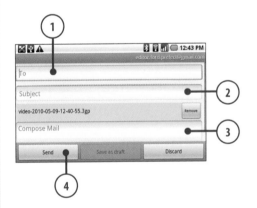

Sharing Video on YouTube

If you have not previously entered your YouTube account, you are prompted to do so before you can upload your video.

1. Enter the title of your video.

2. Enter the description of the video.

3. Set the video's privacy options.

4. Enter any tags for the video, separating tags using commas.

5. Touch Upload.

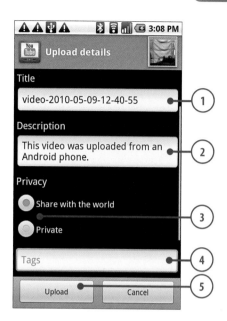

Deleting Videos

1. Touch the Menu button twice to show the Gallery menu.

2. Touch one or more videos. Videos you select have a green check mark.

3. Touch Delete.

4. Touch Confirm Delete.

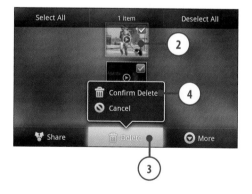

More Details About Your Video

To see more details about a specific video, touch More and then touch Details while the video is selected. The application displays the title, type of video (e.g. 3GPP, MP4), date the video was created, the album it is in, and the GPS location (if this is available).

The Gallery Application—Video (Droid Incredible and Eris)

The Gallery application allows you to view pictures and video, and share pictures and video with people via MMS, Bluetooth, YouTube, and email. We cover viewing and sharing videos in this chapter and cover pictures in Chapter 9.

1. Touch the Gallery icon to launch the Gallery application.

2. Touch the Video or videos' albums to see videos. The Video album contains any video synchronized from your computer; the videos album contains video recorded with the camera on your Droid.

3. Touch a video to start playing it.

4. Touch to return to the albums view.

5. Touch to share the one or more video via Bluetooth, Gmail, Mail, Messages (MMS), or YouTube.

6. Touch to delete one or more videos.

7. Touch to launch the video camera.

8. Drag left and right to move rapidly forward and backward through the video.

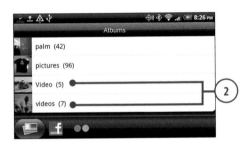

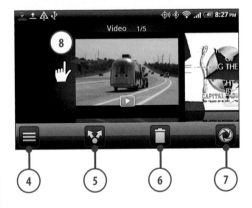

Sharing Videos

You can share small videos with people from the Gallery application. Here
is how.

1. Touch to share one or more
   videos.

2. Touch to choose your method of
   sharing. Remember that if you
   want to share a video on YouTube,
   you must first have a YouTube
   account.

3. Touch one or more videos to
   mark them as selections.

4. Touch Next.

Small Video Size

Depending on your cellular carrier,
you might be able to share only
very small videos from your Droid.
The video file size normally cannot
exceed 3Mb, which is about 1
minute of high-quality video, or
about 2 minutes of low-quality
video. This is true for all types of
video sharing, except MMS,
where the videos can be as short
as 30 seconds.

Bluetooth Sharing Might Fail

Many phones do not accept incoming Bluetooth files, but devices such
as computers do. Even on computers, the recipient must configure
her Bluetooth configuration to
accept incoming files.

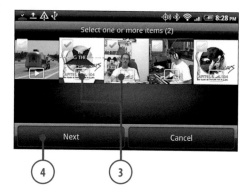

Deleting Videos

1. Touch to select one or more videos for deletion.

2. Touch one or more videos. Videos you select have a red X.

3. Touch Delete.

More Details About Your Video

To see more details about a specific video, touch and hold on a video and then touch Details while the video is selected. The application displays the title, type of video (such as 3GPP or MP4), the date the video was created, the album it is in, and the GPS location (if this is available).

The Gallery Application—Video (Droid X)

The Gallery application enables you to view pictures and video, and share pictures and video with people via MMS, Bluetooth, YouTube, and email. We cover viewing and sharing videos in this chapter and cover pictures in Chapter 9.

1. Touch the Gallery icon to launch the Gallery application.

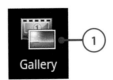

2. Touch the Videos albums to see videos.

3. Touch the Menu button to reveal more options.

4. Touch to launch the video camera.

5. Touch to jump to videos recorded or loaded on a specific day.

6. Touch to select one or more videos.

7. Touch to change the settings of the Gallery application.

8. Drag left and right to move rapidly forward and backward through the video.

9. Touch to start a slide show. This option works only when you are viewing pictures.

10. Touch a video to show it full screen ready for playing. Touch the Play icon on the video to start playing it.

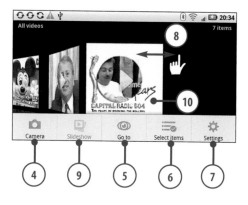

Sharing, Editing, and Deleting Videos

You can share small videos with people from the Gallery application. You can also edit videos right on your Droid including adding titles, shorting the video, and removing frames.

1. Touch the video to show it full screen. Touch the Menu button to reveal more choices.

2. Touch to launch the video camera.

3. Touch to share the video via Bluetooth, Email, Gmail, your online album, MMS, or YouTube.

4. Touch to edit the video. You can add tags to the video or crop it, add titles, or remove frames from it.

5. Touch to delete the video.

6. Touch to change the settings of the Gallery application.

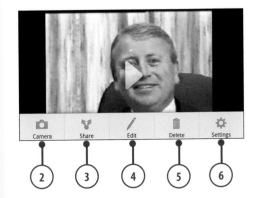

Small Video Size

Depending on your cellular carrier, you might be able to share only very small videos from your Droid. The video file size normally cannot exceed 3Mb, which is about 1 minute of high-quality video, or about 2 minutes of low-quality video. This is true for all types of video sharing, except MMS, where the videos can be as short as 30 seconds.

Bluetooth Sharing Might Fail

Many phones do not accept incoming Bluetooth files, but devices such as computers do. Even on computers, the recipient must configure her Bluetooth configuration to accept incoming files.

Editing Videos

1. Touch a video to show it full screen. Touch the Menu button to reveal more options.

2. Touch to edit the video.

3. Touch to add tags to the video. Tags are like key words.

4. Touch to edit the video.

5. Drag the yellow beginning and end markers to shorten the video.

6. Touch the Menu button to reveal more options.

7. Touch to save the edited video.

8. Touch to extract the current frame from the video.

9. Touch to add a title to the video.

10. Touch to resize the video.

11. Touch to remove the audio from the video.

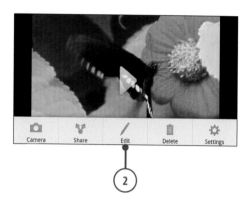

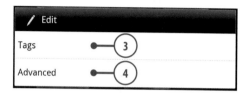

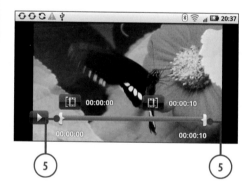

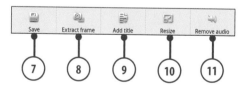

The Camera Application—Recording Videos (Droid 1)

The Camera application enables you to take pictures, record video, and upload video straight to YouTube. We cover the video recording and upload features of the Camera application in this chapter. Using the Camera application to take pictures is covered in Chapter 9.

Recording Video

1. The Camera application should be on the Home screen. Touch to launch it. You can also press and hold the physical Camera button until you feel a short vibration.

2. Slide the switch from the still camera to the video position.

3. Touch the Start Video icon, or press the physical Camera button to start recording video. Touch the icon again or press the trackball again to stop recording.

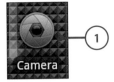

It's Not All Good

VIDEO FOCUSING IS OFF

While the camera is in still camera mode, when you take pictures, your Droid can focus the image using a mechanical auto-focus feature. However while recording videos, the focus remains frozen, so if you bring your Droid too close to someone or something, the video goes out of focus.

Changing Video Settings

Before you record a video, you can change some settings that can alter how the video is recorded.

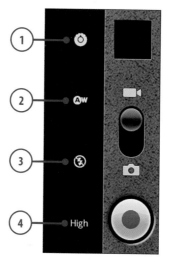

1. Touch to set the color effect. Your choices are Mono, Sepia, Negative, Solarize, Red Tint, Blue Tint, or Green Tint.

2. Touch to set the white balance. Your choices are Incandescent, Daylight, Fluorescent, and Cloudy.

3. Touch to set the flash mode. When in video mode, turning the flash on makes it remain on to light the area while you're recording.

4. Touch to set the video quality. Your choices are High (30m), which is 30 minutes of high-quality video, Low (30m), which is 30 minutes of low-quality video, MMS (Low, 60s), which is 60 seconds of low-quality video for MMS), and YouTube (High, 10m), which is 10 minutes of high-quality video for YouTube.

The Camera Application—Recording Videos (Droid X)

The Camera application enables you to take pictures, record video, and upload video straight to YouTube. We cover the video recording and upload features of the Camera application in this chapter. Using the Camera application to take pictures is covered in Chapter 9.

Recording Video

1. The Camera application should be on the Home screen. Touch to launch it. You can also press and hold the physical Camera button until you feel a short vibration

2. Touch to switch the camera to video mode.

3. Press the physical Camera button to start and stop recording video.

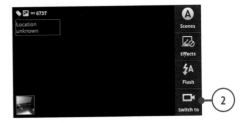

It's Not All Good

VIDEO FOCUSING IS OFF

While the camera is in still camera mode, when you take pictures, your Droid can focus the image using a mechanical auto-focus feature. However while recording videos, the focus remains frozen, so if you bring your Droid too close to someone or something, the video goes out of focus.

Changing Video Settings

Before you record a video, you can change some settings that can alter how the video is recorded.

1. Touch to select scenes. Your choices are Everyday, Outdoors, Concert, Narrative, and Subject.

2. Touch to change the video effects. Your choices are Normal, Black and White, Negative, Sepia, Solarize, Red Tint, Green Tint, and Blue Tint.

3. Touch to turn the light on or off.

4. Touch to switch back to still camera mode.

5. Touch to enable or disable automatic tagging with your GPS location and to add your own custom tags.

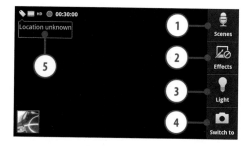

The Camera Application—Recording Videos (Droid Incredible and Eris)

The Camera application enables you to take pictures, record video, and upload video straight to YouTube. We cover the video recording and upload features of the Camera application in this chapter. Using the Camera application to take pictures is covered in Chapter 9.

Recording Video

1. The Camera application should be on the Home screen. Touch to launch it.

2. Touch to pull out the settings panel.

3. Touch to switch the camera to video mode.

4. Press and hold the optical joystick to start recording video. Press it again to stop recording.

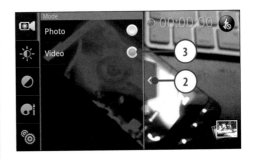

It's Not All Good

VIDEO FOCUSING IS OFF

While the camera is in still camera mode, when you take pictures, your Droid can focus the image using a mechanical auto-focus feature. However while recording videos, the focus remains frozen, so if you bring your Droid too close to someone or something, the video goes out of focus.

Changing Video Settings

Before you record a video, you can change some settings that can alter how the video is recorded.

1. Touch to pull out the settings panel.

2. Touch to change the brightness.

3. Touch to turn the light on or off.

4. Touch to change the contrast, saturation, and sharpness.

5. Touch to choose video effects. Your choices are Gray Scale, Sepia, Negative, Solarize, and Posterize.

6. Touch to change the video settings including White Balance, ISO, Resolution, and Widescreen On/Off.

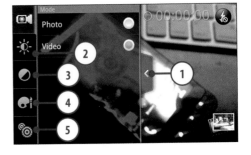

YouTube

Your Droid comes with a YouTube application that enables you to find and watch videos, rate them, add them to your favorites, and share links to YouTube videos. The YouTube application even enables you to upload new videos.

YouTube Main Screen

1. Touch the YouTube icon on the Home screen to launch the application.

2. Touch to play a video.

3. Touch to see information about the video and related videos.

4. Touch to upload your own video.

5. Touch to search for videos.

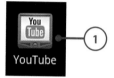

Playing a Video

While playing a YouTube video, you can rate the video, read video comments, and share the video with someone.

1. Touch to see details about the video, and see related videos.

2. Touch to rate the video. This still uses the old-style five-star rating system. It is likely that the YouTube application will be updated to support the new YouTube rating system soon.

3. Touch to read comments about this video. You cannot add your own comments.

4. Touch to add the video to your YouTube favorite video list.

5. Touch to share the video with people using MMS, email, and Facebook. When you share the video, you are sharing only the link to it.

6. Touch More to flag a video as inappropriate or switch to another version of the video (either high or low quality).

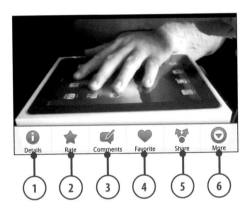

Filtering Videos

When you first open the YouTube application, you are presented with the Featured videos. You can view videos from a specific category only.

1. Touch the Menu button, and touch Categories.

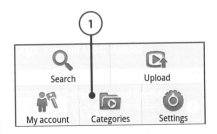

2. Scroll to and touch a category you want to filter the view to. Videos that have been uploaded today under this category are displayed.

3. Touch the Menu button and touch Time Filter to see videos older than today.

4. Touch the time filter you want. The Category display updates. When you change the time filter, it affects all YouTube screens.

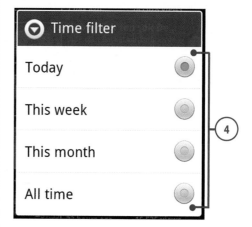

Changing YouTube Settings

If you want to clear your YouTube search history, or change the time filter, you can do this in the YouTube application's settings screen.

1. Touch the Menu button while looking at the main YouTube screen, then touch Settings.

2. Touch to clear your YouTube searches.

3. Touch to set the time filter.

Amazon MP3

Your Droid comes with the Amazon MP3 application. This application enables you to search for and purchase music from Amazon and download it directly to your phone. Before you start, you need an Amazon account. If you don't have one, visit Amazon.com on your desktop computer to sign up.

Setting Up the Amazon MP3 Application

After you have your Amazon.com account, you are ready to use Amazon MP3. Here is how to set it up by entering your account details.

1. Touch the Amazon MP3 Store icon on the home screen.

2. Touch the Menu button after you see the main Amazon MP3 screen, and then touch Settings.

3. Touch to clear the Amazon application's cache. The cache is actually useful because it keeps copies of images and other content that helps screens load quicker, but clearing the cache can free up memory.

4. Touch to enable and disable connection monitoring. Keeping this enabled is a good idea because it allows the Amazon application to resume music downloads if you go into a cellular dead spot.

5. Touch to let the Amazon MP3 application remember your Amazon login.

6. Touch to access your Amazon account, or type in your details if this is your first time running the application.

7. Enter the email address you used to sign up with Amazon.com.

8. Touch OK to save your login information.

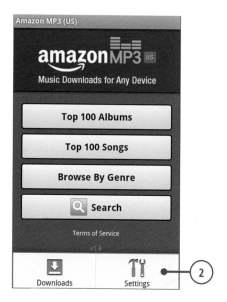

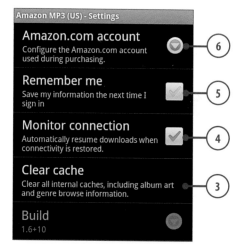

Finding Music

1. Touch to see the top 100 albums.

2. Touch to see the top 100 songs.

3. Touch to browse by music genre.

4. Touch to search for music.

Purchasing Music

After you find what you are looking for, you can preview the song and then purchase it.

1. Touch a song to listen to 30 seconds of it.

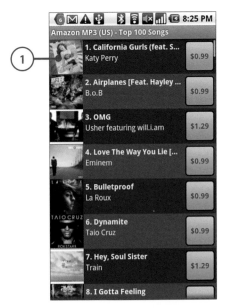

2. Touch the price to purchase the song. The price changes to the word BUY. Touch BUY to continue.

3. Enter your Amazon.com password. Your email address should already be there.

4. Touch OK. Your song or album is then downloaded.

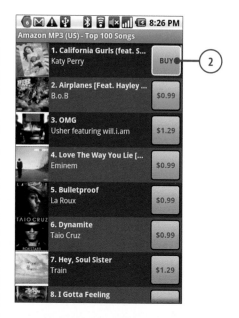

Using doubleTwist to Synchronize Audio and Video

You might already have a large music collection on your computer and maybe some movies and videos you want to copy over to your Droid. You can use a free program called doubleTwist to do this. We went through the steps of installing and setting up this application in the Prologue. If you haven't installed it yet, skip back to the Prologue and follow the instructions.

Running doubleTwist and Mounting Your Droid

When you use doubleTwist, you need to connect your Droid to your computer using the supplied USB cable and mount it as a new drive. Get started by launching doubleTwist on your computer and connecting your Droid via the USB cable.

1. Pull down the notification bar and touch USB Connected.

2. Touch Turn on USB Storage.

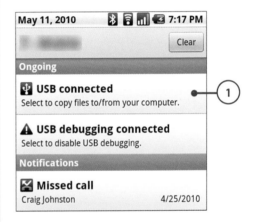

3. On the Droid X, touch USB Mass Storage and touch OK. On the HTC Incredible and Eris, touch Disk Drive and touch Done. Now your Droid displays under DEVICES in doubleTwist.

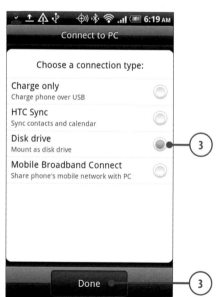

Synchronizing Music by Dragging It

After your Droid is visible in doubleTwist, you can drag music to it.

1. Click Music in doubleTwist to see all the music on your computer.

2. Find the song you want to drag to your Droid.

3. Click and drag it down to your Droid under DEVICES. You should see a green plus icon when your mouse is hovering over your Droid. When you drop the song on your Droid, doubleTwist copies it over.

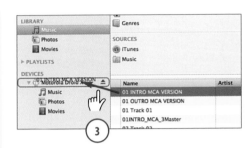

Synchronizing Existing Playlists

If you have iTunes installed, you might have already created playlists of music. You can use doubleTwist to synchronize those playlists.

1. Click your Droid under DEVICES.

2. On the right of the screen, you see any existing playlists. Put a check mark next to Sync Music.

3. Put a check mark next to any playlists you want to synchronize to your Droid.

4. Click Sync.

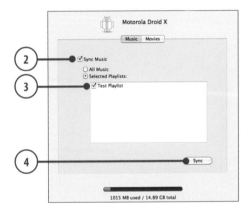

Sync All Music

You can choose to synchronize all music, but if your music collection is large, it might not fit on your Droid. Remember that all music and video is copied to the Micro-SD card you insert under the battery cover, so the more music you want to synchronize, the larger that memory card needs to be.

Creating Playlists

If you are using iTunes to synchronize playlists, then you can create new playlists in iTunes and use doubleTwist to synchronize the music. However if you don't use iTunes, or you want to create playlists outside of iTunes, you can create them in doubleTwist.

1. Click the new Playlist button in doubleTwist.

2. Type the name of your new playlist.

3. Find music on your computer in the Music section of doubleTwist.

4. Drag that music to your newly created playlist. When you've added songs to the playlist, repeat the steps in the "Synchronize Existing Playlists" section to move the playlist to your Droid.

Using doubleTwist with the Amazon MP3 Music Store

You can use the Amazon MP3 Music store on your Droid to purchase music, but you can also access it in doubleTwist.

1. Click on Music Store under the DOUBLETWIST heading and then click Sign In.

2. The first time you try to use doubleTwist to purchase music from Amazon, you see a warning telling you to sign in to your Amazon account using a web browser. Click Go To Amazon.com to continue.

3. Complete the process online. When complete you see a confirmation message in doubleTwist. Click Continue to use the Music Store.

Copying Video

Normally, you need to manually convert your video to work on mobile devices. This involves figuring out the screen size and CODECs to use. doubleTwist has a great feature that automatically converts the video for you as you drag it onto your Droid.

1. Click Movies under DOUBLETWIST. Find the video or movie you want to copy to your Droid.

2. Drag the video to your Droid. If the video is in your iTunes archive, even if it has no DRM, you won't be able to drag and drop it.

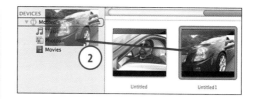

3. A pie chart indicator shows the progress of the video conversion. After the pie chart fills up, it disappears to indicate that the video has been successfully moved.

In this chapter, you learn about your Droid's connectivity capabilities including Bluetooth, Wi-Fi, VPN, and web browsing. Topics include the following:

4

→ Pairing with Bluetooth devices
→ Connecting to Wi-Fi networks
→ Virtual Private Networks (VPN)
→ Using your Droid as a Wi-Fi Hotspot

Connecting to Bluetooth, Wi-Fi, and VPNs

Your Droid can connect to Bluetooth devices such as headsets, computers, and car in-dash systems, as well as to Wi-Fi networks, and 2G and 3G cellular networks. It has all the connectivity you should expect on a great Smartphone. Your Droid can also connect to virtual private networks (VPN) for access to secure networks. Some Droids can even share their 3G cellular connection with other devices over Wi-Fi.

Connecting to Bluetooth Devices

Bluetooth is a great personal area network (PAN) technology that allows for short distance wireless access to all sorts of devices such as headsets, other phones, computers, and even car in-dash systems for hands free calling. The following tasks walk you through pairing your Droid to your device and configuring options.

Pairing with a New Bluetooth Device

Before you can take advantage of Bluetooth, you need to connect your Droid with that device, which is called pairing. After you pair your Droid with a Bluetooth device, they can connect to each other automatically in the future.

1. Touch the Menu button, and then touch Settings.

2. Touch Wireless & Networks.

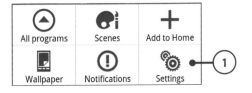

3. Touch to enable Bluetooth.

4. Touch Bluetooth Settings.

5. Touch Device Name to change the name that your Droid uses when it broadcasts on the Bluetooth network.

6. Touch Discoverable if you want to make your Droid discoverable on the Bluetooth network. Your Droid remains discoverable for 120 seconds (2 minutes). Making your Droid discoverable is necessary when someone else is trying to pair with your Droid.

7. Touch to enable the Droid Incredible Bluetooth FTP server. When this is enabled, you can drag and drop files to and from your Droid Incredible and a desktop computer without having to connect it using the USB cable.

8. Touch Scan for Devices to get your Droid to scan the Bluetooth network for other Bluetooth devices. If your Droid finds any other devices, they are listed on the screen. In this example, a Bluetooth headset and a computer were found.

9. To pair with a Bluetooth device, touch the device. In this example, we are pairing with the Plantronics headset.

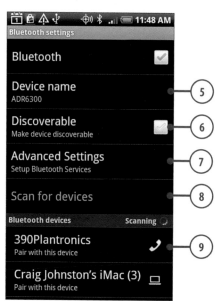

Droid X Enhanced Stereo

If you have a Droid X, on the Bluetooth settings screen, you will see an extra option called Enhanced Stereo. If you enable this, when you pair your Droid X with compatible stereo Bluetooth devices that supports Stereo Bluetooth Class 1.5, Version 2.1 + EDR, you should hear enhanced audio quality when playing MP3 files, plus it improves the battery life of your Droid X.

10. If you are pairing with a device that requires a passkey, such as a car in-dash system or a computer, the screen shows a passkey. Make sure the passkey is the same on your Droid and on the device you are pairing with. Touch Pair on your Droid, and confirm the passkey on the device you are pairing with.

11. If all went well, your Droid should now be paired with the new Bluetooth device.

All Zeros

If you are pairing with an older Bluetooth headset, you might be prompted to enter the passkey. Try using four zeros as the passkey. It normally works. If the zeros don't work, refer to the headset's manual.

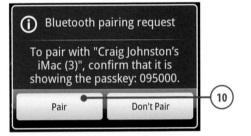

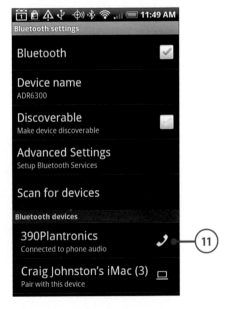

Changing Bluetooth Options

After a Bluetooth device is paired, you can change a few options for some of them. The number of options depends on the Bluetooth device you are connecting to. Some have more features than others.

1. Touch and hold on a Bluetooth device to see available options.

2. Touch to disconnect from the Bluetooth device.

3. Touch to disconnect and unpair from the Bluetooth device. If you do this, you won't be able to use the device until you redo the pairing as described in the previous task.

4. Touch for more options.

5. Touch to connect with the Bluetooth device, if you are currently disconnected from it.

6. Touch to enable and disable using this device for phone calls. Sometimes Bluetooth devices have more than one profile. You can use this screen to select which ones you want to use.

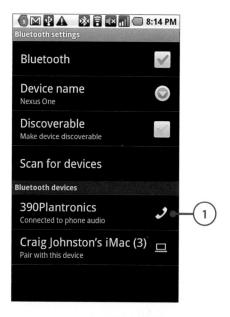

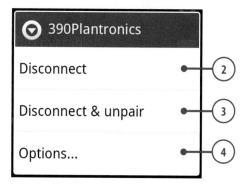

Bluetooth Profiles

Each Bluetooth device can have one or more Bluetooth profiles. Each Bluetooth profile describes certain features of the device. This tells your Droid what it can do when connected to it. A Bluetooth headset normally only has one profile such as Phone Audio. This tells your Droid that it can only use the device for phone call audio. Some devices might have this profile but provide other features such as Phone Book Access profile which would allow it to synchronize your Droid's address book. The latter is typical for car in-dash Bluetooth.

Quick Disconnect

To quickly disconnect from a Bluetooth device, touch the device on the Bluetooth Settings screen and then touch OK.

Wi-Fi

Wi-Fi (Wireless Fidelity) networks are wireless networks that run within free radio bands around the world. Your local coffee shop probably has free Wi-Fi, and so do many other places such as airports, train stations, malls, and other public areas. Your Droid can connect to any Wi-Fi network and provide you higher Internet access speeds than the cellular network.

Connecting to Wi-Fi

The following steps explain how to find and connect to Wi-Fi networks. After you have connected your Droid to a Wi-Fi network, you automatically are connected to it the next time you are in range of that network.

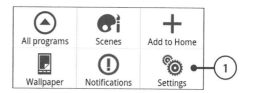

1. Touch the Menu button and touch Settings.

2. Touch Wireless & Networks.

3. Touch to enable Wi-Fi.

4. Touch to change Wi-Fi Settings and connect to Wi-Fi networks.

5. Touch to turn on or off your Droid's Wi-Fi radio.

6. Touch Network Notification to enable or disable the notification that tells you a new open Wi-Fi network is available.

7. Touch a Wi-Fi network to connect to it.

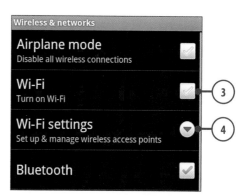

8. If the Wi-Fi network is secure, you receive a prompt to enter a password or encryption key.

9. Touch to show the password or encryption key characters as you type them.

10. Touch Connect to continue.

11. If all goes well you see the Wi-Fi network in the list with the word Connected under it.

Can't Connect to Wi-Fi?

If all does not go well, you might be typing the password or encryption key incorrectly. Verify this with the person who owns the Wi-Fi network. Sometimes there is a lot of radio interference that causes problems. Ask the person who owns the Wi-Fi network to change the channel it operates on and try again.

Wi-Fi Network Options

1. Touch a Wi-Fi network to reveal a pop-up that shows information about your connection to that network.

2. Touch Forget to tell your Droid to not connect to this network in the future.

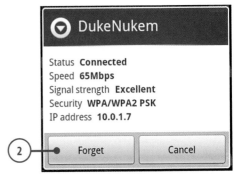

3. Touch and hold on a Wi-Fi network to reveal two actions.

4. Touch to forget the Wi-Fi network and no longer connect to it.

5. Touch to change the Wi-Fi network password or encryption key that your Droid uses to connect to the network.

Advanced Wi-Fi Options

Your Droid allows you to configure a few advanced Wi-Fi settings that can actually help preserve your battery life.

1. Touch the Menu button while on the Wi-Fi Settings screen and touch Advanced.

2. Touch Use Static IP to force your Droid to use a static IP address and static network access settings.

3. Use this Wi-Fi MAC address if you need to provide a network administrator with your MAC address in order to be able to use a Wi-Fi network.

4. Touch to change the Wi-Fi sleep policy.

5. Choose when you want your Droid's Wi-Fi radio to go to sleep.

Wi-Fi Is More Efficient

Believe it or not, Wi-Fi is more efficient than a 3G cellular network. The more time you can keep the Wi-Fi radio on and connected to a Wi-Fi network, the longer your battery will last. If you have a valid data connection via Wi-Fi, your Droid actually stops using the cellular 3G network. So, while at home, why not set the Wi-Fi sleep policy to Never.

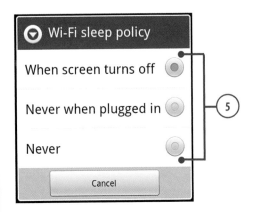

>>> Go Further

WHY USE A STATIC IP OR MAC?

Firstly what are an IP address and a MAC address? A MAC address is a number burned into your Droid that identifies its Wi-Fi adapter. This is called the physical layer because it is a physical adapter. An IP address is a secondary way to identify your Droid. Unlike a physical layer address or MAC address, the IP address can be changed anytime. Modern networks use the IP address when they need to deliver some data to you. Typically when you connect to a network, a device on the network assigns you a new IP address. On home networks, this is typically your Wi-Fi router.

In rare circumstances, the Wi-Fi network you connect to might not assign your Droid an IP address. In these circumstances, you will need to ask the network administrator to give you a static IP address.

Some network administrators use a security feature to limit who can connect to their Wi-Fi network. They set up their network to allow only connections from Wi-Fi devices with specific MAC addresses. If you are trying to connect to such a network, you will have to give the network administrator your MAC address, and he will add it to the allowed list.

Cellular Networks (GSM)

Your Droid can connect to 2G (GPRS), 2.5G (EDGE), and 3G (UMTS/HSDPA) cellular networks.

Changing Mobile Settings

Your Droid has a few options when it comes to how it connects to cellular (or mobile) networks.

1. Touch the Menu button and touch Settings.

2. Touch Wireless & Networks.

3. Touch Mobile Networks.

4. Touch Data Roaming to set whether your Droid connects to data while you are roaming outside your home carrier's network.

5. Touch to see the name of the carrier you are connected to and any access point names (APN). You can also manually add APNs if you want.

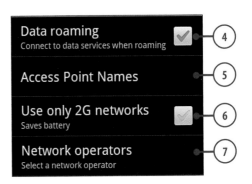

What Is an APN?

APN stands for Access Point Name. You normally don't have to make changes to APNs but sometimes you need to enter them manually to access certain features. For example, if you need to use tethering, which is where you connect your laptop to your Droid and your Droid provides Internet connectivity for your Droid, you might be asked by your carrier to use a specific APN. Think of an APN as a gateway to a service.

6. Touch Use Only 2G Networks to tell your Droid to not use the 3G cellular radio. Using only 2G extends the life of your battery, but it makes Internet access slow.

7. Touch Network Operators to select a network operator or carrier to connect to.

8. Touch to search for mobile networks.

9. Touch to set your Droid to automatically select a mobile network.

10. Touch a mobile network to force your Droid to only connect to that specific network.

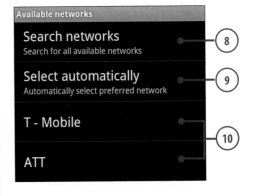

How Does Automatic Roaming Work?

You should leave your Droid to automatically select a mobile network. It always connects to your wireless provider first. For example if you have a T-Mobile SIM card, your Droid always tries to connect to T-Mobile first. If it can't, it attempts to connect to the next best network. When you roam to other countries, your Droid still tries to connect to your wireless provider, but it if is not found the Droid chooses a local provider for you. Sometimes your provider might not have a roaming agreement with the carrier that your Droid has chosen, and this is when you'd want to set it to manual and select the network yourself.

Cellular Networks (CDMA - Verizon)

Your Verizon Droid can connect to 2G (CDMA 1X) and 3G (EVDO Rev A) cellular networks.

Changing Mobile Settings

Your Droid has a few options when it comes to how it connects to cellular (or mobile) networks.

1. Touch the Menu button and touch Settings.

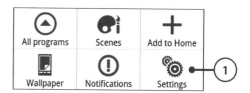

2. Touch Wireless & Networks.

3. Touch Mobile Networks.

4. Touch Data Roaming to set whether your Droid connects to data while you are roaming outside your home carrier's network.

5. Touch to enable or disable playing a sound when you connect to a roaming network.

6. Touch to enable to disable always-on mobile data. It is advisable to leave this enabled otherwise your Droid is not able to update anything such as weather, news, email, and other things that update over the wireless network.

7. Touch to change the roaming mode. You can set the roaming mode to Home only, which means the Droid does not connect to other CDMA networks, or Automatic, which enables the Droid to connect to any CDMA network.

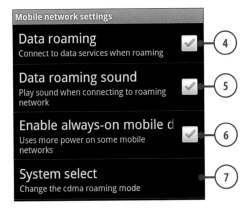

It's Not All Good

ROAMING TO OTHER COUNTRIES

Unfortunately, all of the Verizon Droids can only operate on CDMA networks. Most countries use GSM, which means that it is unlikely that you will be able to travel abroad with your Droid. This is quite limiting because it means that you need to rent a GSM phone or go without your Droid on trips.

Virtual Private Networks (VPN)

Your Droid can connect to virtual private networks (VPNs), which are normally used by companies to provide a secure connection to their inside networks or intranets.

Adding a VPN

Before you add a VPN, you must first have all the information needed to set it up on your Droid. Speak to your network administrator and get this information ahead of time to save frustration. This information includes the type of VPN protocol used, type of encryption used, and the name of the host to which you are connecting.

1. Touch the Menu button and touch Settings.

2. Touch Wireless & Networks.

3. Touch VPN Settings.

4. Touch to add a new VPN.

5. Touch the VPN technology your company uses.

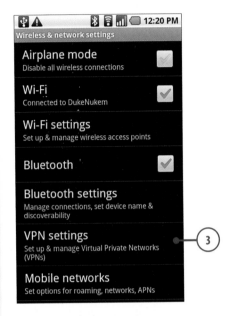

6. Go through each section and enter the information your network administrator gave you.

7. Touch Save to save the VPN settings.

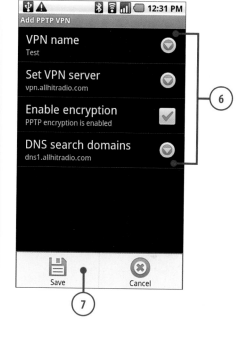

Connecting to a VPN

After you have created one or more VPN connections, you can connect to them when the need arises.

1. Follow steps 1–3 in the "Adding a VPN" section to navigate to the VPN Settings screen.

2. Touch the VPN you want to connect to.

3. Enter your username and password.

4. Touch Connect. After you're connected to the VPN, you can use your Droid's web browser and other applications normally, but you now have access to resources at the other end of the VPN tunnel, such as company web servers or even your company email.

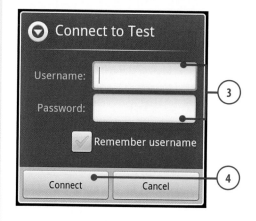

3G Mobile Hotspot

The Droid X and Droid Incredible (with the FroYo update) have an application called 3G Mobile Hotspot that enables you to use Wi-Fi to share your Droid's 3G Internet connection with up to five devices. This feature works only with an optional extra monthly fee, which covers the extra data you use when this feature is enabled.

Setting Up and Starting Your 3G Mobile Hotspot (Droid Incredible)

If you have a Droid Incredible, which has been updated to Android 2.2 (FroYo) you can use 3G Mobile Hotspot. Here is how to set it up and start it.

1. Touch to launch 3G Mobile Hotspot.

2. Enter a unique name for the Wi-Fi network you create when you enable this feature.

3. Touch to select the type of security you want to use on the Wi-Fi network, or select no security. It is a good idea to use security so that the people who connect to your Hotspot have encrypted data going over the air.

4. Enter the password or key you want to use on your Hotspot to encrypt the data.

5. Touch to start your Mobile Hotspot.

6. Anyone who wants to share your cellular 3G connection to the Internet needs to scan for your Wi-Fi Hotspot, connect to it, and enter the password.

>> Go Further

ADVANCED HOTSPOT SETTINGS

Most of the time you need to only follow the steps in this task to set up and start your 3G Mobile Hotspot, but if you want to change the way that the Hotspot works, you need to go to the Advanced screen. To do this, touch the Menu button and touch Advanced. On the Advanced screen you can change the channel that your Wi-Fi Hotspot uses. This is useful if there are other Wi-Fi networks nearby that seem to be interfering with yours. The LAN settings enable you to set the IP address, Subnet mask, decide whether to use DHCP, and determine what IP address DHCP must start with. The Power mode enables you to change how your Wi-Fi Hotspot behaves when there is no activity on the Wi-Fi network. You can set it to disable itself after 5 or 10 minutes of inactivity, or always stay on.

Setting Up and Starting Your 3G Mobile Hotspot (Droid X)

If you have a Droid X that has been updated to Android 2.2 (FroYo) you can use 3G Mobile Hotspot. Here is how to set it up and start it.

1. Touch to launch 3G Mobile Hotspot.

2. Press the Menu button and touch Advanced to first set up your Hotspot.

3. Touch to change the settings of your Hotspot.

4. Enter a unique name for the Wi-Fi network you create when you enable this feature.

5. Touch to select the type of security you want to use on the Wi-Fi network, or select no security. It is a good idea to use security so that the people who connect to your Hotspot have encrypted data going over the air.

6. Enter the password or key you want to use on your Hotspot to encrypt the data.

7. Touch to change the channel your Wi-Fi Hotspot uses. Sometimes if there are other Wi-Fi Hotspots around using the same channel, they can interfere with yours, which degrades the speed. Changing the channel can eliminate that interference.

8. Touch to Save your settings and return to the previous screen.

9. Press the Back button to return to the main screen.

10. Touch to start your Mobile Hotspot.

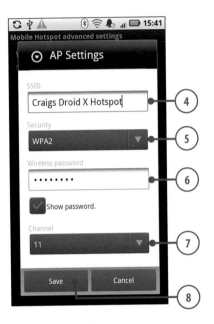

It's Not All Good

NO BLUETOOTH WHILE USING HOTSPOT

If you use the Droid X's 3G Mobile Hotspot application, when you start the Hotspot, it disables Wi-Fi and Bluetooth. This means that while using the Hotspot feature, you are no longer able to use any Bluetooth devices such as headsets. Even worse, when you stop the Hotspot, your Droid X does not re-enable Wi-Fi or Bluetooth, leaving you to enable them both manually. The Droid Incredible does not have this issue.

HotSpot Sucks Power

When you use 3G Mobile Hotspot, it is a good idea to keep your Droid plugged in to the wall or to a car charger. This is because 3G Mobile Hotspot uses a lot of power and CPU cycles and drains your battery very quickly.

In this chapter, you learn about your Droid's email applications for Gmail and other email accounts such as POP3, IMAP, and even Microsoft Exchange. Topics include the following:

→ Adding a Gmail account

→ Adding a Microsoft Exchange account

→ Sending and receiving email

→ Working with attachments

Emailing

Your Droid has two email programs: the Gmail application, which works only with Gmail, and the Mail application that works with POP3, IMAP, and Microsoft Exchange accounts. Both email clients are pretty well rounded although the Exchange support area is lacking.

Gmail

When you first set up your Droid, you set up a Gmail account. The Gmail application enables you to have multiple Gmail accounts, which is useful if you have a business account and a personal account.

Adding a Gmail Account

When you first set up your Droid, you added your first Gmail account. The following steps describe how to add a second account.

1. Touch the Gmail icon on the Home screen.

2. Touch the Menu button and touch Accounts.

3. Touch Add Account. After this, if you have a Droid Incredible or Droid Eris, you see a screen with Google. Touch it to continue. If you have a Droid X, you see a screen with multiple types of accounts listed. Touch Google to continue.

4. Touch Next.

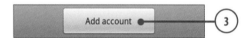

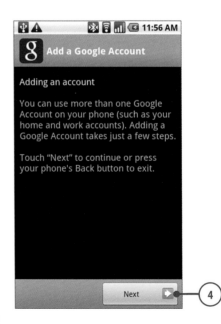

5. Choose whether you want to add an existing Gmail account or create a new one.

6. If you chose to add an existing Gmail account, enter your Google username and password.

7. Touch Sign In. If you already have a Gmail account, skip to step 22.

8. If you chose to add a new Gmail account, type in your first and last name.

9. Type your desired Gmail email address.

10. Touch Next to continue.

11. If the Google account (Gmail email address) you chose is already taken, you see a screen suggesting alternatives. Select an alternative account name or type a new one and touch Next.

12. Type a password for your new Google account. The stronger the password is, the longer the Password Strength line becomes.

13. Retype the password in the Confirm Password box.

14. Touch Next.

15. Choose a security question.

16. Type the answer.

17. Type in a secondary email address, which should be an existing email address.

18. Touch Create.

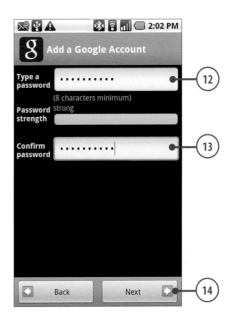

19. Touch I Agree, Next.

20. Type in the characters that match the captcha image.

21. Touch Next.

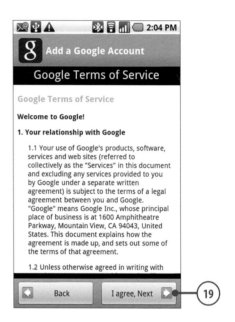

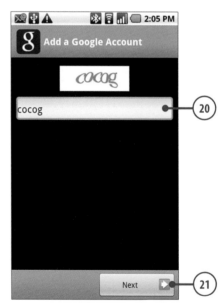

22. Choose what to synchronize to your Droid.

23. Touch Finish.

Why Multiple Gmail Accounts?

You are probably wondering why you would want multiple Gmail accounts. Isn't one good enough? Actually it is not that uncommon to have multiple Gmail accounts. It can be a way to compartmentalize your life between work and play. You might run a small business using the one account but email only friends with another. Your Droid supports multiple accounts but still allows you to interact with them in one place.

Composing Gmail Email

Now that you have at least one Gmail account set up, you can start sending and receiving email using one of the Gmail accounts.

1. If you have more than one Gmail account, touch the account you want to use.

2. Touch the Menu button and touch Compose.

3. Type names in the To field. If the name matches someone in your Contacts, the name is displayed and you can touch it to select it.

4. Enter a subject.

5. Type a message.

6. If you want to add a picture as an attachment to the email, touch the Menu button and touch Attach.

7. Touch the picture you want to attach.

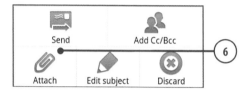

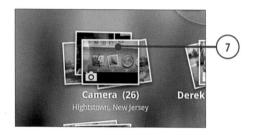

Only Picture Attachments

Even though you might have some short video clips and documents on your Droid, you are unable to select them as attachments. Hopefully this will be addressed in a future release of Android.

---

8. Touch Save as Draft to store the email in the Drafts folder.

9. Touch Discard to get rid of the email completely.

10. Touch to send the email.

Reading Gmail Email

It seems obvious enough, but this section covers how to handle attachments and a few other tricks.

1. Touch an email to open it.

2. Touch to add the sender to your Contacts.

3. Touch to download the attachment. This downloads and saves the attachment on your Droid.

4. Touch to preview the attachment. This does not download or save it.

5. Touch to archive the email.

6. Touch to delete the email.

7. Touch to see the previous email in your inbox.

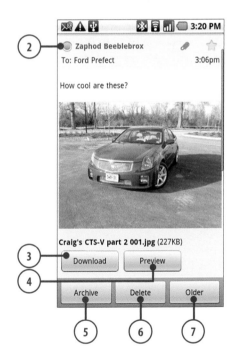

8. Scroll down to the bottom of the email to see three actions you can take on the email. Touch to reply to the sender only.

9. Touch Reply to All to reply to the sender and all other recipients of the email.

10. Touch to forward the email to someone.

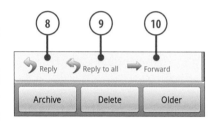

11. Touch the Menu button to see more choices. Touch Newer to move to the next email in your inbox.

12. Touch to add a star to the email.

13. Touch Mark Unread to return the email to unread status.

14. Touch to change labels. Labels are Gmail's name for folders.

15. Touch Back to Inbox to return to the inbox view.

16. Touch More for more options.

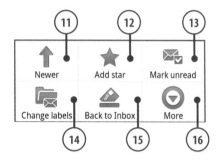

STARS AND LABELS

>>> Go Further

Gmail allows you to use stars and labels to help organize your email. In most email clients you can create folders in your Inbox to help you organize your emails. For example you might create a folder called "emails from the boss" and move any emails you receive to that folder. Gmail doesn't use the term folders; it uses the term labels instead. You can create labels in Gmail and choose an email to label. When you do this, it actually moves it to a folder with that label, but to you, the email has a label distinguishing it from other emails. An email that you mark with a star is actually just getting a label called "starred." But when viewing your Gmail, you see the yellow star next to an email. People normally add a star to an email as a reminder of something important.

17. Touch Mute to block emails from this sender.

18. Touch to report this email as spam.

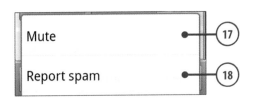

What Happens to Your SPAM?

When you mark an email in Gmail as SPAM, two things happen. Firstly it gets a label called Spam. Secondly a copy of that email is sent to Gmail's Spam servers, so they are now aware of a possible new Spam email that is circulating around the Internet. Based on what the servers see for all Gmail users, they block that Spam email from reaching other Gmail users. So the bottom line is, always mark Spam emails as Spam because it helps all of us.

Gmail Settings

You can customize the way Gmail accounts work on your Droid by changing the email signature and choosing which labels synchronize.

1. While you have the inbox of the account you want to change settings for, touch the Menu button and touch Settings.

2. Touch to change the email signature.

Email Signature

An email signature is a bit of text that is automatically added to the bottom of any emails you send from your Droid. It is added when you compose a new email, reply to an email, or forward an email. A typical use for a signature is to automatically add your name and maybe some contact information at the end of your emails. Email signatures are sometimes referred to as email footers.

3. Touch Confirm Delete to enable or disable confirmations when you're deleting emails.

4. Touch Batch Operations to enable or disable the ability to select more than one message when working with labels.

5. Touch to clear your search history.

6. Touch Labels to choose which labels to synchronize. Labels are what Gmail calls folders.

7. Touch Email Notifications to enable or disable notifications in the status bar when new email arrives for this account. Scroll down to see more options.

8. Touch Select Ringtone to choose the ringtone that plays when new email arrives for this account.

9. Touch Vibrate to enable or disable vibration when new email arrives for this account.

Setting Up the Email Application

In addition to the Gmail application that works only with Gmail, there is a second email application that handles Microsoft Exchange, POP3, and IMAP email accounts. POP3 and IMAP are typically used by online email hosts, whereas Microsoft Exchange is used mostly by businesses. The email application can normally set up accounts automatically, but sometimes you have to use the manual process, especially when adding Microsoft Exchange accounts.

Adding a New Microsoft Exchange Account (Droid 1 and 2)

If you use your Droid as your only phone, you might want to have both personal and corporate email on it. If this is first time using the email application, you are prompted to set up an account. Because we are going to set up an Exchange account, we use the manual process.

1. Type in your corporate email address.

2. Type in your corporate network password.

3. Touch Manual Setup.

4. Touch Microsoft Exchange ActiveSync.

5. Type in your corporate domain name, a backslash, and your corporate username.

6. Type in your corporate network password.

7. Type in your corporate ActiveSync server.

8. Touch to enable or disable the use of SSL. This is almost always enabled.

9. Touch Next.

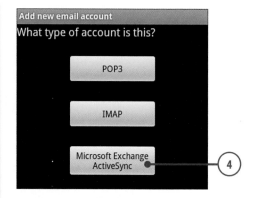

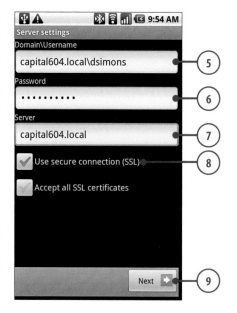

10. Touch to change the email delivery frequency. Typically this is left at Automatic (Push), which means as email arrives in your corporate inbox, it arrives on your Droid.

11. Touch to change how far back email is synchronized. You can synchronize as far back as one month.

12. Touch to enable or disable making this your default account when sending email from your Droid.

13. Touch to enable or disable notifications when email arrives for this account.

14. Touch to enable or disable synchronizing contacts with this account. If you leave this enabled, your Outlook contacts synchronize to your Droid.

15. Touch Next.

16. Type a name for this account.

17. Type your name as you would like it to be displayed when you send email from this account.

18. Touch Done.

Exchange Account Settings (Droid 1 and 2)

After you set up an Exchange ActiveSync account, you can change the way it functions on your Droid.

1. While the Exchange inbox is open, touch the Menu button and touch Settings.

2. Touch Account Name to change the account's name.

3. Touch Your Name to change the way your name is displayed when you send email from this account.

4. Touch Email Check Frequency to change how often server is checked for new messages.

5. Touch Amount to Synchronize to change the time period for which email is synchronized.

6. Touch Default Account to enable or disable this account as being the default account when new email is composed in the Email application.

7. Touch Email Notifications to enable or disable notifications in the status bar when new email arrives. Scroll down to see more options.

8. Touch Select Ringtone to change the ringtone that plays when new email arrives for this account.

9. Touch Vibrate to enable or disable vibration when new email arrives for this account.

10. Touch Incoming Settings to change the Exchange ActiveSync server settings.

11. Touch Sync Contacts to enable or disable Outlook contacts synchronization.

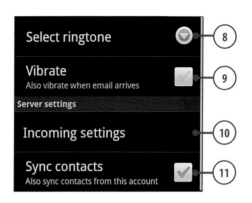

Adding a New POP3 or IMAP Account (Droid 1 and 2)

Before we cover how to use the Email application, let's add a POP3 or IMAP account. These are typically used by hosted email systems such as Yahoo! or Hotmail.

1. From the accounts screen, touch the Menu button and choose Add account.

2. Type your email address.

3. Type your email account's password.

4. If you are using a common, well-known hosted email system such as Yahoo! or Hotmail, touch Next and the Email application should figure out the rest automatically.

5. If you are not using a common host email system, touch Manual Setup.

>>> Go Further

WHY MANUAL?

Your Droid tries to figure out the settings to set up your email account. This works most of the time when you are using common email providers such as Yahoo! or Hotmail and others. It also works with large ISPs such as Comcast, Road Runner, Optonline, and so on. It might not work for smaller ISPs, or in smaller countries, or if you have created your own web-site and set up your own email. In these cases, you need to set up your email manually.

6. Touch the type of email account you are using. Everyone supports POP3, but many now support IMAP. If your system supports both, select IMAP as it is much more flexible than POP3.

7. Type in your username for the mail account. This is normally your full email address.

8. Type in your password.

9. Type in the server name for incoming mail. Because I had chosen POP3, I've used my POP3 server name.

10. Change the incoming mail server port number if necessary.

11. Touch to select the type of security being used.

12. Touch to choose when emails you delete on your Droid are also deleted on your mail server.

13. Touch Next.

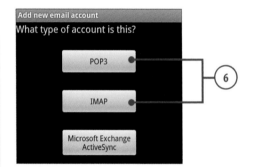

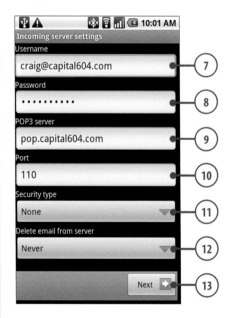

Where Can I Find This Information?

If you need to manually set up your email account, you must have a few pieces of information. Always check your ISP's, or email service provider's, website, and look for instructions on how to set up your email on a computer or Smartphone. This is normally under the support section of the website.

14. Type the server name for your outgoing mail.

15. Change the server port for outgoing mail if necessary.

16. Touch to change the security type used.

17. Touch to enable or disable the need to sign in to your outgoing mail server each time you need to send email.

Username and Password

On this screen, your username and password should already be filled out because you typed them in earlier. If not, enter them now.

18. Touch Next.

Be Secure If You Can

If your mail provider supports email security such as SSL or TLS, you should strongly consider using it. If you don't, emails you send and receive go over the Internet in plain readable text. Using SSL or TLS encrypts the emails as they travel, so nobody can read them.

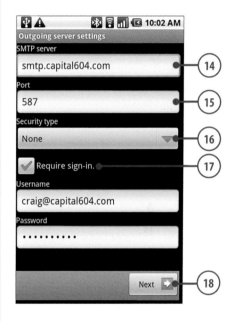

19. Touch to change how frequently the application checks for new email. The less frequently you check, the more battery life you experience.

20. Touch to enable or disable this account as the default account used to send new emails.

21. Touch to enable or disable notification when new email arrives for this account.

22. Touch Next.

23. Type a name for this account.

24. Type your name as you want it displayed when you send new emails from this account.

25. Touch Done.

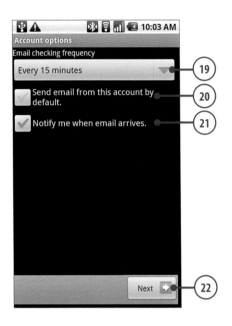

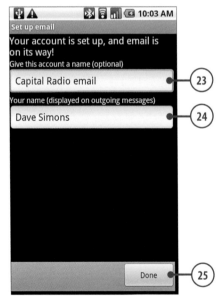

Working with the Email Application (Droid 1 and 2)

Now that we have added two new accounts, we can start using the Email application. Everything you do in the email application is the same for every email account.

Using Combined or Separate Inboxes

The Email application allows you to work with your different email accounts separately, or in a combined Inbox.

1. Touch the Menu button and touch Accounts to see a list of all accounts you have configured.

2. Touch an individual account to see only its Inbox.

3. Touch the Folder icon to see the folders for that account.

4. A check mark signifies which account is the default account.

5. Touch Combined Inbox to see all email accounts' inboxes merged into one view.

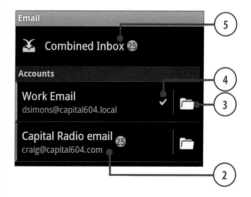

6. When in the combined inbox view, emails from different accounts have different colors. This helps to visually separate them from one another. In this example, orange represents our Exchange emails and blue represents our POP3 emails.

7. A black background indicates an email has already been read.

8. A gray background indicates an unread email.

9. Touch the check marks to select multiple messages and work with them as a group.

10. Touch to add a star to a message. This is like flagging the message.

Composing Email

No matter if you are looking at the combined inbox or a separate account's inbox, composing email is the same.

1. Touch the Menu button and choose Compose.

No Corporate Name Search

There is currently no way to search your corporate address book from your Droid. This means that you need to know the email address of anyone you want to email at your company, unless you add them to your Outlook Contacts.

---

2. Type in the recipients. If the Droid recognizes names you type as being in your Contacts, you see a list of names to choose from. Commas need to separate recipients' addresses, but luckily the application adds them for you. If you type in an address manually, when you hit space, a comma is added. If you select an address, a comma is added.

3. Type a subject.

4. Type a message.

5. Touch Discard to cancel the message.

6. Touch Save as Draft to store the message in the Drafts folder.

7. Touch to send the message. Touch the Menu button to see additional options for the message.

8. Touch Add Cc/Bcc to copy or blind copy certain addresses on the message.

9. Touch to add one or more attachments. Remember you can attach only pictures.

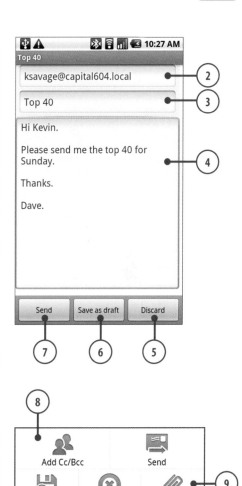

Reading Email

Reading messages in the Email application is the same regardless of which account the email has come to.

1. Touch an email to open it.

2. Touch to add the sender to your contacts.

3. Touch to add a star to a message. This is like flagging a message.

4. Touch the Open button to view an attachment. This previews only the attachment and does not save it.

5. Touch to save an attachment to your Droid.

6. Touch to reply only to the sender.

7. Touch to reply to the sender and any other recipients.

8. Touch to delete the email. Touch the Menu button to see more options.

9. Touch to forward the message.

10. Touch to mark the message as unread.

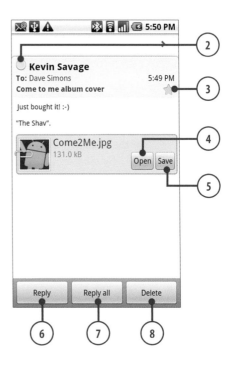

Adding a New Microsoft Exchange Account (Droid Incredible and Eris)

If you use your Droid as your only phone, you might want to have both personal and corporate email on it. If this is your first time using the email application, you are prompted to set up an account. Because we are going to set up an Exchange account, we use the manual process. The Droid Incredible and Eris use an application called Mail for all non-Gmail email.

1. Touch to launch the Mail application.

2. Touch Exchange ActiveSync.

3. Touch Manual Setup.

4. Enter your corporate email address.

5. Enter your company's ActiveSync server address. It's normally mail.<YourCompany'sDomain>.com.

6. Enter your company's Active Directory Domain name. The Domain name is normally displayed on the login screen of your company's computers.

7. Enter your network username. This is the username you use every day to log in to your company's network.

8. Enter your network password. This is the password you use every day to log in to your company's network.

9. Touch to enable or disable the use of SSL. This is almost always enabled.

10. Touch Next.

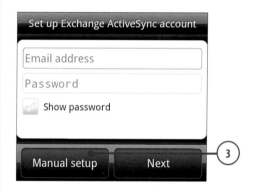

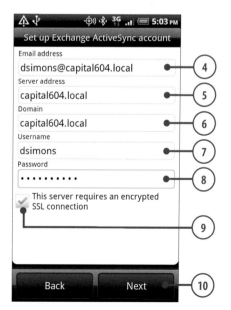

11. Touch to enable or disable syn-
    chronization of Mail, Contacts, and
    Calendar. Most people leave these
    as enabled.

12. Touch Finish Setup.

Exchange Account
Settings (Droid Incredible
and Eris)

After you set up an Exchange
ActiveSync account, you can change
the way it functions on your Droid.
For example you might want it to
synchronize more email.

1. While the Exchange inbox is
   open, touch the Menu button and
   touch More.

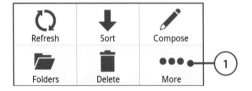

2. Touch Settings.

3. Touch to edit the account settings, such as changing the password.

4. Touch to set the font size, set your email signature, and choose where to save attachments (internal, phone, or SD card).

5. Touch to choose how much of an email to download, the email format (HTML or text), whether emails arrive in real-time or on a schedule, how much past email to download, and whether to download email attachments.

6. Touch to change how you are notified when new email arrives.

7. Touch to delete the account from your Droid.

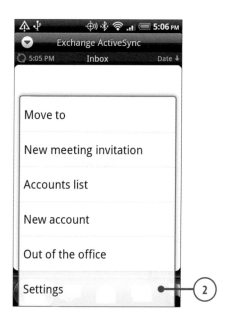

Setting Your Out of Office Message (Droid Incredible and Eris)

With the Droid Incredible and Eris, you can set your Out of Office message and enable or disable it. This synchronizes back to Outlook, so you can truly set it while on the road.

1. While the Exchange inbox is open, touch the Menu button and touch More.

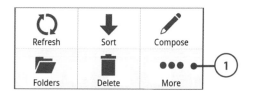

2. Touch Out of the Office.

3. Touch to select whether you are in or out of the office.

4. Set the start and end date and time when you will be out of the office.

5. Type your out of office message.

6. Touch save and set your out of office message.

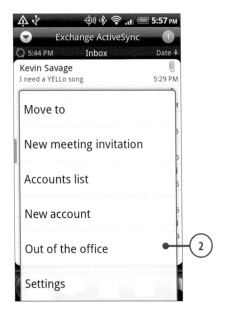

Adding a New POP3 or IMAP Account (Droid Incredible and Eris)

Before we cover how to use the Email application, let's add a POP3 or IMAP account. These are typically used by hosted email systems such as Yahoo! or Hotmail.

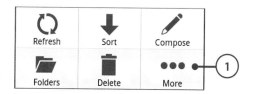

1. From the accounts screen, touch the Menu button and touch More.

2. Touch New Account.

3. Touch Manual Setup.

Why Manual?

Your Droid tries to figure out the settings to set up your email account. This works most of the time when you are using common email providers such as Yahoo! or Hotmail and others. It also works with large ISPs such as Comcast, Road Runner, Optonline, and so on. It might not work for smaller ISPs, in smaller countries, or if you have created your own website and set up your own email. In these cases, you need to set up your email manually.

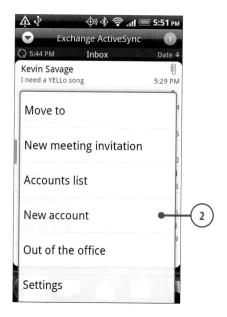

4. Touch to change the protocol used by your email service. Everyone supports POP3, but many now support IMAP and APOP. If your system supports APOP, choose it over POP because it does not send your password in clear text. If your system supports IMAP, select it as it is much more flexible than POP and APOP.

5. Enter your email address.

6. Enter your username. Many systems use your full email address as your username.

7. Enter your password.

8. Enter POP server. You can get this information from your email host.

9. Choose the type of security used, if any.

10. Touch to change the server port used. Most email hosts leave this at the default value.

11. Touch Next.

Be Secure If You Can

If your mail provider supports email security such as SSL or TLS, you should strongly consider using it. If you don't, emails you send and receive go over the Internet in plain readable text. Using SSL or TLS encrypts the emails as they travel so that nobody can read them.

12. Touch to name your account, or leave it set as your email address. You could use a name like Personal email to distinguish it from your office email.

13. Enter your full name. Don't leave it as your email address.

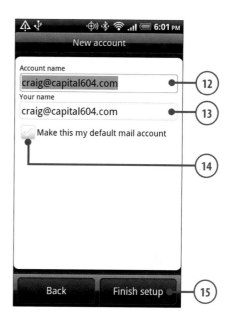

Where Can I Find This Information?

If you need to manually set up your email account, you must have a few pieces of information. Always check your ISP's, or email service provider's, website, and look for instructions on how to set up your email on a computer or Smartphone. This is normally under the support section of the website.

14. Touch to make this your default account. Do this if you want to use this account anytime you compose a new email.

15. Touch Finish Setup.

Working with the Email Application (Droid Incredible and Eris)

Now that we have added two new accounts, we can start using the Email application. Everything you do in the email application is the same for every email account.

Navigating the Main Screen

The Mail application has multiple views and can switch between email accounts so that you can keep your work and home email separated.

1. Touch to switch between email accounts.

2. Touch an email to read it.

3. Touch to see the Conversations view. This view is useful if there has been a lot of back and forth on a certain email. As long as the original subject line hasn't changed, this view shows you the entire email conversation.

4. Touch to view or edit your favorite contacts.

5. Touch to view only unread email.

6. Touch to view only emails that have been flagged.

7. Indicates an urgent email.

8. Indicates that the email has one or more attachments.

9. Indicates that the email is unread.

10. Indicates how many emails are unread.

11. Indicates that an email is flagged.

Composing Email

No matter which mail account you are working with, composing email is the same.

1. Touch the Menu button and choose Compose.

2. Type in the recipients. If the Droid recognizes names you type as being in your Contacts, you see a list of names to choose from. Commas need to separate recipients' addresses, but luckily the application adds them for you. If you type in an address manually, when you hit space, a comma is added. If you select an address, a comma is added.

3. Touch to search for recipients on your corporate network.

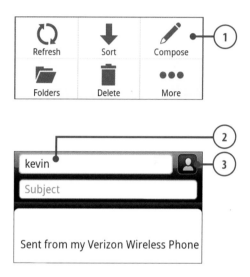

It's Not All Good

CORPORATE NAME SEARCH IS KLUDGY

The Droid Incredible and Eris have a kludgy way of searching for corporate contacts. Unlike other Droids that search your corporate directory as you type someone's name into the To field, these Droids make you perform a multi-step process.

4. Touch to search your corporate directory.

5. Type part of a name.

6. Touch to search.

7. Touch one or more names from the return list to select them as recipients.

8. Repeat steps 5–7 for multiple names.

9. Touch OK to return to the email.

10. Type a subject.

11. Type your email.

12. Touch the Menu button to reveal more message options.

13. Touch to save the message as a draft. This saves it in your Drafts folder.

14. Touch to discard the message.

15. Touch to show the Cc and Bcc fields.

16. Touch to set the message priority to High, Normal, or Low.

17. Touch to add one or more attachments. You can attach pictures, video, audio, an application recommendation, your current GPS location, or a document.

18. Touch Send to send the email.

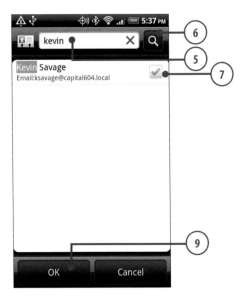

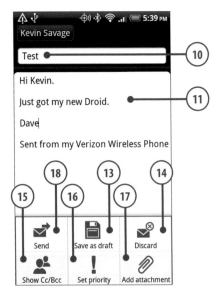

Reading Email

Reading messages in the Email application is the same regardless of which account the email has come to.

1. Touch an email to open it.

2. Touch to reveal all recipients.

3. Touch to flag a message. Flagging messages helps remind you that the message is important or that you need to respond to the sender.

4. Touch the reveal any attachments.

5. Touch an attachment to download it. After it has downloaded, touch it again to open it.

6. Touch to reply only to the sender.

7. Touch to reply to the sender and any other recipients.

8. Touch to move to the next email (older).

9. Touch to move to the previous email (newer).

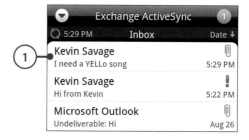

10. Touch the Menu button to reveal more options.

11. Touch to return to the received messages view.

12. Touch to the conversations view, highlighting this message in that view.

13. Touch to compose a new message.

14. Touch to mark the message you are reading as unread.

15. Touch to delete the message you are reading.

16. Touch to forward the message.

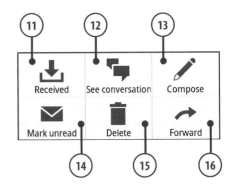

Adding a New Microsoft Exchange Account (Droid X)

If you use your Droid as your only phone, you might want to have both personal and corporate email on it. If this is your first time using the email application, you are prompted to set up an account. Because we are going to set up an Exchange account, we use the manual process.

1. Touch to launch the Email application.

2. Touch the Menu button and touch Manage Accounts.

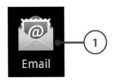

3. Touch Add Account.

4. Touch Corporate Sync.

5. Enter your network username preceded by your company's Active Directory Domain name and a backslash. You normally see this domain name on your company computer's login screen.

6. Enter your network password.

7. Enter your email address.

8. Enter Exchange ActiveSync server name. This is normally mail.< YourCompany'sDomainName> .com.

9. Touch to enable or disable the use of SSL. This is almost always enabled.

10. Touch Next.

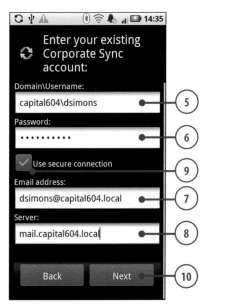

11. Touch to complete the setup.

Success!

Messaging + Calendar + Contacts

With a Corporate Sync account, your contacts, calendar and emails are wirelessly synchronized with this device. You can choose to sync all three types of data or any combination.

Access your Corporate Sync Inbox in the universal Messaging app. New emails appear in your inbox automatically.

The Motorola Messaging widget also shows the latest unread text messages, emails, and social networking messages all together in a single stream -- or you can pick and choose accounts.

Done ⎯⎯11

Adding a New POP3 or IMAP Account (Droid X)

Before we cover how to use the Email application, let's add a POP3 or IMAP account. These are typically used by hosted email systems such as Yahoo! or Hotmail.

1. From the main Email screen, touch the Menu button and touch Manage Accounts.

2. Touch Add Account.

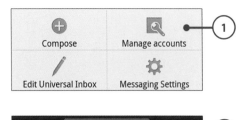

⊕ Compose	🔍 Manage accounts ⎯⎯1
✎ Edit Universal Inbox	⚙ Messaging Settings

Add account ⎯⎯2

3. Touch Email.

4. Enter your email address.

5. Enter your password.

6. Touch to unselect Automatically Configure Account, unless you are confident that your Droid will be able to figure it out.

7. Touch Next.

Why Manual?

Your Droid tries to figure out the settings to set up your email account. This works most of the time when you are using common email providers such as Yahoo! or Hotmail and others. It also works with large ISPs such as Comcast, Road Runner, Optonline, and so on. It might not work for smaller ISPs, in smaller countries, or if you have created your own website and set up your own email. In these cases, you need to set up your email manually.

8. Touch to change the name of the account, your name as you want it displayed when sending emails, and the email address.

9. Touch to change the protocol used by your email service, the name of your incoming mail server, and your login information if required.

Which Protocol to Use

Everyone supports POP3, but many now support IMAP. If your system supports IMAP, select it as it is much more flexible than POP (also known as POP3).

10. Touch to enter your outgoing mail server information, and your login information if required.

11. Touch OK to complete the setup.

Be Secure If You Can

If your mail provider supports email security such as SSL or TLS, you should strongly consider using it. If you don't, emails you send and receive go over the Internet in plain readable text. Using SSL or TLS encrypts the emails as they travel so nobody can read them.

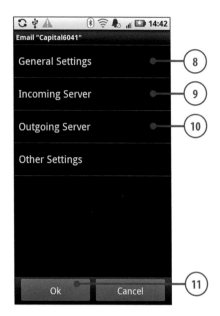

Where Can I Find This Information?

If you need to manually set up your email account, you must have a few pieces of information. Always check your ISP's, or email service provider's, website, and look for instructions on how to set up your email on a computer or Smartphone. This is normally under the support section of the website.

Working with the Email Application (Droid X)

Now that we have added two new accounts, we can start using the Email application.

Navigating the Main Screen

The Droid X's Email application enables you to view all of your email accounts in a Universal Inbox, or you can view emails separately.
Everything you do in the email application is the same for every email account.

1. Touch to view all accounts in one universal view, called the Universal Inbox.

2. Touch an individual account to see just messages for that account.

3. Touch to compose a new message.

4. Indicates how many draft messages you have.

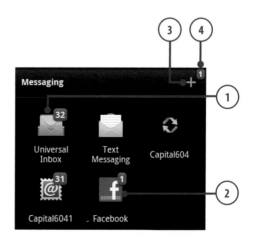

Universal Inbox (Droid X)

The Universal Inbox lists SMS and MMS messages and emails in all configured accounts, including online accounts like Facebook. Let's take a look.

1. Touch to open the Universal Inbox.

2. Touch to compose a new message.

3. Touch to read a message.

4. Indicates an unread message.

5. Indicates an Exchange email.

6. Indicates a Facebook email.

7. Indicates an MMS message.

8. Indicates a POP3 or IMAP message.

9. Touch to select one or more messages to move or delete.

10. Touch to manually refresh the Universal Inbox.

11. Indicates the message is flagged.

12. Indicates the message has one or more attachments.

13. Indicates the message is urgent.

Universal Inbox Account Settings (Droid X)

When you modify the settings for the Universal Inbox, you modify them for all accounts. Let's take a look.

1. With the Universal Inbox open, touch the Menu button and touch Settings.

2. Touch to modify settings for text (SMS) and multimedia (MMS) messaging.

3. Touch to modify settings for all email accounts including Exchange and POP3/IMAP.

4. Touch to modify settings for social networking accounts such as Facebook and MySpace.

5. Touch to modify settings for emergency alert services. This includes Presidential Alerts (which cannot be disabled), Extreme Alerts, Severe Alerts, and AMBER Alerts.

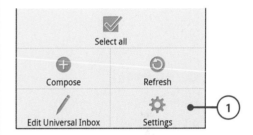

Modifying Which Accounts Universal Inbox Shows

Universal Inbox is a great way to keep all account Inboxes in one view; however, you might not want to include every Inbox. Here is how to select the Inboxes that are displayed.

1. With the Universal Inbox open, touch the Menu button and touch Edit Universal Inbox.

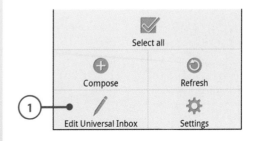

2. Touch to select and unselect which accounts are included in the Universal Inbox view.

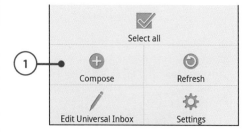

Composing Email

No matter which mail account you are working with, composing email is the same.

1. Touch the Menu button and choose Compose.

2. Touch to select which account you are composing the message for.

3. Start typing the names of the recipients. Your Droid searches for matches in your Contacts as well as in your corporate directory.

4. Touch a matching contact to add it to the To field.

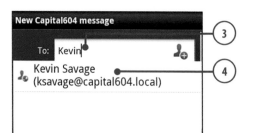

5. Press Enter when you have added all of the recipients. This enables you to move to the Subject and body portions of the email.

6. Type the body of the message.

7. Touch to make characters bold, italic, or underlined.

8. Touch to start a bulleted list. Touch again to end the bulleted list.

9. Touch to add an emoticon (for example, a smiley face).

10. Type to see font properties and colors.

11. Touch to choose a font.

12. Touch to choose the size of the text.

13. Touch to choose the color of the text.

14. Touch to choose the text background color.

15. Touch to send the message.

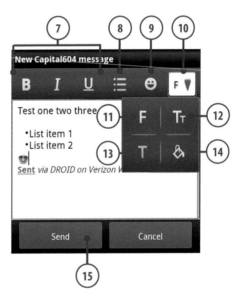

16. Touch the Menu button to reveal more options.

17. Touch to return to the Inbox view.

18. Touch to add one or more attachments. You can add pictures, video, music, or audio from the Sound Recorder.

19. Touch to add Carbon Copy (CC) recipients.

20. Touch to add Blind Carbon Copy (BCC) recipients. BCC recipients get the email but the other recipients don't see the names of the BCC recipients.

21. Touch to set the importance of the email.

22. Touch to see more choices.

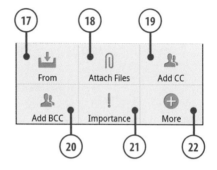

23. Touch to hide the text formatting toolbar. Touch again to unhide the toolbar.

24. Touch to change the email account settings.

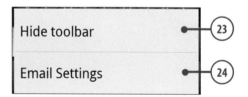

Reading Email

Reading messages in the Email application is the same regardless of which account the email has come to.

1. Touch an email to open it.

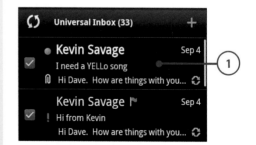

2. Touch to reveal all recipients.

3. Touch an attachment to download it. After it has downloaded, touch it again to open it.

4. Touch to reply only to the sender or forward the message.

5. Touch to delete the message.

6. Touch a name to see information about the person, add the information to an existing contact, or add the person to your contacts.

7. Press the Menu button to reveal more choices.

8. Touch to move the message to a folder.

9. Touch to mark the message as unread.

10. Touch to flag the message.

In this chapter, you learn about browsing the World Wide Web and using the browser capabilities of your Droid. Topics include the following:

→ Bookmarking websites

→ Sharing websites with your friends

→ Keeping track of sites you have visited

→ Using GPS and browsing together

Browsing the Web

Your Droid has a fully featured web browser for a smartphone. The experience using the Droid's browser is similar to using a desktop browser, just with a smaller screen. You can bookmark sites, hold your Droid sideways to fit more onto the screen, and even share your GPS location with sites.

Navigating with the Browser

Let's dive right in and cover how to run the browser and use all of its features. Your Droid's browser can be customized, shares your GPS location, enables you to bookmark sites, and keeps your browsing history.

1. Touch Browser on the Home screen. On some Droids, this icon is called Internet.

2. Touch to type in a new web address. Some websites move the web page up to hide the address field. When this happens, you can drag the web page down to reveal the address bar again.

3. Touch a link to follow it.

4. Touch to see the browser bookmarks. (See the next section for information on setting bookmarks.)

Alternate Bookmarks Location

On some models of Droid such as the HTC Droid Eris and HTC Droid Incredible, this icon is not there. To reach the bookmarks on these models, touch the Menu button and then touch Bookmarks.

5. Double-touch a section of the web page to instantly zoom into it. Double-touch to zoom back out.

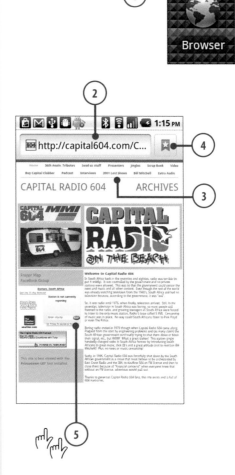

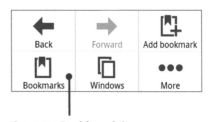

On some Droid models, touch the Menu button and then touch Bookmarks

6. Use your thumb and index finger to zoom in and out of a web page. Pinching your thumb and index finger together zooms out, whereas moving them apart zooms in.

7. Rotate your Droid onto its side to view the web page in landscape mode.

Managing Bookmarks

Bookmarks are a great way to save
your favorite websites in one place
so that you can just jump right back
to them.

1. Touch the Bookmarks icon to see
   your bookmarks. The Bookmarks
   screen displays thumbnails repre-
   senting each website that you
   have bookmarked.

2. Touch a bookmark to load that
   website.

3. You can switch the Bookmarks
   screen from a Thumbnail view to
   a List view by touching the Menu
   button, and then touching List
   View.

4. Touch and hold a bookmark to
   reveal the bookmark actions
   menu.

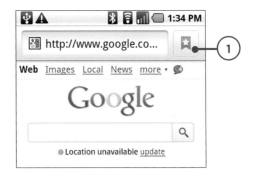

An Alternative Thumbnail View

On some Droids, there are three Bookmark views: Grid, Thumbnail, and List. On these Droids, the Grid view is the same as the Thumbnail view on other Droids. The Thumbnail view on these Droids is different because it creates thumbnails on a single line that you drag left or right with your finger.

Thumbnails are on a single line. Drag left or right to browse them

5. Touch to open the bookmark.

6. Touch to open the bookmark in a new window.

7. Touch to edit the bookmark.

8. Touch Add Shortcut to Home to add the bookmark to your Droid's Home screen. This enables you to jump to the bookmark without having to first launch the browser.

9. Touch to share the bookmark with your friends using email, Facebook, Gmail, or Messaging.

10. Touch Copy Link URL to copy the bookmark's address. You can then paste this address into another screen.

11. Scroll down to see more options.

12. Touch to delete the bookmark.

13. Touch Set as Homepage to make this bookmark your browser's Home page. The Home page is the page that loads when you first open the browser.

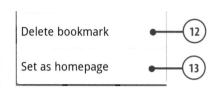

Using GPS Location

Your Droid has a built-in GPS radio that enables it to tell exactly where it is on planet Earth. If you allow websites to see this information, they can become even more useful.

1. If you visit a website that requests your location, touch Share Location.

Website requests your location

2. In this example, which uses the Google home page, the website knows my location, and it gives me options to find restaurants, coffee shops, bars, and ATMs near me.

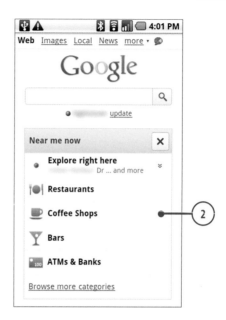

Navigating with the Navigation Pad, Trackball, and Optical Joystick

Sometimes links on web pages are too small to touch with your finger. Your Droid has an alternative navigation method that can assist in these circumstances. This is a navigation pad on the Droid, optical joystick on the Droid Incredible, and trackball on the Droid Eris.

1. Move your finger on the pad, trackball, or joystick to move an orange cursor between all the links on a web page.

2. Press the pad, trackball, or joystick to select a link.

Pad/Trackball/ Joystick cursor

3. Press and hold the pad, trackball, or joystick to bring up a menu with more choices for that link.

4. Scroll with the pad, trackball, or joystick to the choice you want and press.

Managing Multiple Windows

Your Droid can have multiple web pages open at one time, each in a different window. Here is how to open and work with multiple windows.

1. Touch the Menu button to reveal the window options.

2. Touch New Window to add a new browser window.

3. Touch Windows to view a list of the open browser windows.

On the Windows screen, you can do the following:

4. Touch New Window to add a new window.

5. Touch a window name to switch to that window.

6. Touch the X icon next to a window name to close the window.

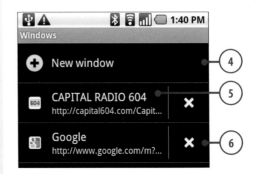

Setting Page Options

While you are viewing a page, you
can perform a number of tasks
including selecting and copying text,
and finding text on the page. To see
the options, touch the Menu button
while viewing a web page.

1. Touch More.

2. Touch to add a bookmark for this
   page.

3. Touch Find on Page to search for
   text on the page.

4. Enter the text you want to find
   and touch Done.

5. Touch to select text and copy it to
   the clipboard.

6. Touch to view page information,
   such as the page name and
   address.

7. Touch to share the page with your
   friends using Bluetooth, email,
   Facebook, Gmail, or Messaging.

8. Touch Downloads to view the
   downloads queue. This is the
   queue of any files that you downloaded while using the browser.

9. Touch Settings to customize the
   browser settings. See the next
   task for more on the browser
   settings.

Customizing Browser Settings

Your Droid's browser is customizable. Here are the different settings you can adjust.

1. Touch the Menu button and touch More.

2. Touch Settings.

3. Touch Text Size to change the text size used when rendering web pages. Choices range from Tiny to Huge. The default is Normal.

4. Touch to change the default zoom level when opening web pages. Choices are Far, Medium, and Close. The default zoom is Medium.

5. Touch Open Pages in Overview to turn off page overview. Page overview is when a page appears zoomed out to an overview of the page, as opposed to the page being viewed at 100% zoom.

6. Touch Text Encoding to choose a different encoding option. Use this to select text encoding for Japanese and other characters.

7. Touch to block pop-up windows. Pop-up windows are almost always advertisements, so keeping this enabled is a good idea; however, some websites might require that you turn off pop-up blocking.

8. Touch Load Images to enable or disable image loading. When Load Images is disabled, the browser loads web pages with no images, which makes the pages load faster.

9. Touch Auto-Fit Pages to make web pages automatically fit the screen horizontally.

10. Scroll down to see more settings.

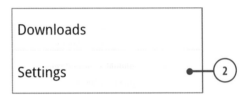

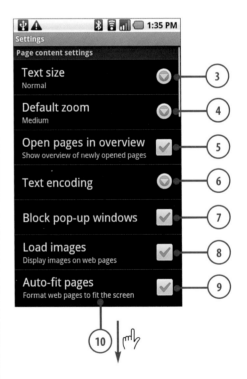

11. Touch Landscape-Only Display to force all web pages to display in landscape mode.

12. Touch to enable or disable JavaScript. JavaScript is used on many web pages for formatting and other functions, so you might want to leave this enabled.

13. Touch to enable or disable browser plug-ins. Plug-ins enhance the standard functionality of the browser.

14. Touch Open in Background to force loading new windows in the background. When this is enabled, a new window does not automatically become the current window; you have to switch to it to make it the current window.

15. Touch Set Home Page to manually set the browser home page to the current web page, or type in any web page address.

16. Touch to clear the browser cache. The browser cache is used to store data and images from websites you visit so that the next time you go back, some of the web page can be loaded straight out of memory.

17. Scroll down to see more options.

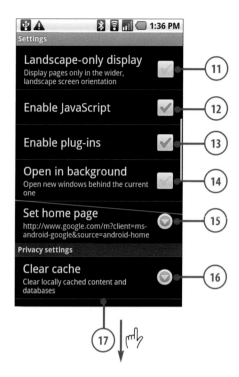

18. Touch to clear your browser history. This clears the history of websites you have visited on your Droid.

19. Touch Accept Cookies to enable or disable accepting cookies. Browser cookies are used by websites to personalize your visit by storing information specific to you in the cookies.

20. Touch to clear all cookie data. This wipes out all locally stored cookies.

21. Touch Remember Form Data to enable or disable remembering form data. Form data is information you enter into forms on web pages, such as your name, phone number, or email address. When you enable this feature you can automatically fill in fields on forms.

22. Touch to clear all previously entered web form data.

23. Touch Enable Location to enable or disable the ability for websites to access your GPS information.

24. Touch to clear location settings for all websites you have visited.

25. Scroll down to see more options.

26. Touch Remember Passwords to enable or disable the browser's ability to remember the usernames and passwords you enter on different websites.

27. Touch to clear any passwords you have previously entered while on websites.

28. Touch Show Security Warnings to enable or disable website security warnings. Your Droid can warn you if a website you are visiting appears to have a security violation of some kind.

29. Touch Reset to Default to return the browser to the out-of-the-box state and clear all browser data.

30. Touch Website Settings to see settings for specific websites you've visited.

31. Touch a website to see its settings.

32. Touch to disable this website's ability to see your GPS location.

33. Touch Clear Access.

34. Touch the Back button to return to the web page.

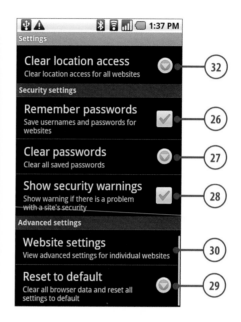

Indicates website can use GPS location information | Website saved cache level

It's Not All Good

FLASH

Some current Droids, and some that will get an upgrade to Android 2.2 in the future, support Adobe Flash in a limited form. This version of Flash is limited to some of the full version's functions, so don't expect all Flash content to work. For example, if you go to CNN's home page and click the video, it won't work.

Flash uses a lot of computing power, which is why many smartphones don't support it. More computing power means more battery drain. In the browser settings, you can disable Flash support.

>> Go Further

MOBILE BROWSING

Some Droids have an extra browser setting for disabling any mobile versions of websites (versions that are formatted for mobile devices). This usually means that the version is stripped down. Websites can figure out if you are using a mobile or desktop device based on your Browser Agent information that is sent each time you request a web page. Based on that information, the website might redirect you to the mobile version.

Modern mobile browsers can handle regular websites just fine, and so-called mobile versions of the sites are not needed. The setting modifies the Browser Agent information so that it appears that you are browsing from a desktop computer, and therefore you always see the regular website and never the mobile version.

Uncheck to disable Flash support

> ⚠ ⇕   ⊕ 🛜 ..∎ 🔋 12:32 PM
> **Settings**
> **Home page configuration**
> **Set home page**   ⊙
> http://www.google.com/m?client=ms-
> android-verizon
> **Display configuration**
> **Load images** ☑
> Display images on web pages
> **Load Flash** ☑
> Display Flash on web pages
> **Block pop-up windows** ☑
> **Mobile view** ☑
> Enable mobile versions of web pages
> **Enable JavaScript** ☑
> Open in background

Uncheck to always show the real website

Downloading Files

While browsing the Web, you might want to download files to your Droid. These could be video or audio files, or even documents and applications.

1. Touch and hold on a picture or link for an object you would like to download.

2. Touch Save Link.

3. The downloads screen and the progress of the download display.

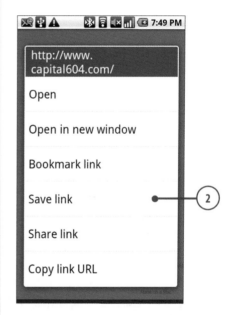

4. After the download has completed, touch the file to view or play it.

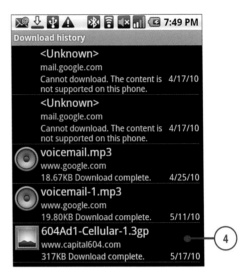

Reviewing History and Most Viewed Sites

Your Droid's browser keeps track of all web pages you visit. Because of this it allows you to find those sites using two screens, Most Viewed and History.

Most Viewed

Most viewed websites are assigned their rankings based on how often you view each one over time.

1. Open the browser and touch the Bookmarks icon. On some Droids, such as the Droid Incredible, you need to touch Menu and then Bookmarks.

2. Touch Most Viewed. All websites that you have visited are ranked with the most visited on top. On some Droids, such as the Droid Incredible, the icon for Most Viewed is a heart; the icons are at the bottom of the screen.

3. Touch a website name to load it.

History

The History screen retains all websites that you have visited and groups them by date. This is useful if you want to find a website you know you visited on a particular date but can't remember the exact address.

1. Open the browser window and touch the bookmarks icon.

2. Touch History. On some Droids, such as the Droid Incredible, the icons are at the bottom of the screen.

3. Touch a category to expand it and see the websites you visited on that day.

4. Touch a website to visit the website.

5. Touch the Menu button and then touch Clear History to clear all traces of your web browsing history.

In this chapter, you learn how to work with text and multimedia messages. Topics include the following:

→ Creating text and multimedia messages
→ Attaching files to multimedia messages
→ Saving received multimedia attachments
→ Working with text messages on your SIM card

Text and Multimedia Messaging

Short Message Service (SMS), also known as text messages, have been around for a long time and are still used today as the primary form of communication for many younger phone users. Multimedia Message Service (MMS) is a newer form of text messaging that can contain pictures, audio, and video. Your Droid is at the top of its game when it comes to SMS and MMS.

The Messaging Application

The Messaging application is what
you use to work with SMS and MMS.
This application has all the features
you need to compose, send, receive,
and manage these messages. Let's
take a look at the main screen.

1. Touch Messaging on the Home
   screen. The main screen of the
   Messaging application shows a
   list of message threads. Touch the
   Menu button to reveal more
   choices.

Messaging on Droid X

If you have a Droid X, the
Messaging application has some
extra features. When you open
Messaging on a Droid X, you are
presented with three choices:
Universal Inbox, Text Messaging,
and Facebook. Facebook is your
Facebook Inbox, Text Messaging
contains SMS and MMS messages,
and Universal Inbox is all three in
one view. To follow the steps this
section, touch Text Messaging.

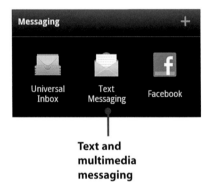

Text and
multimedia
messaging

Messaging on Droid Incredible

If you have a Droid Incredible, the Messaging application has some extra features. When you open Messaging on a Droid Incredible you are presented with the All Messages view. If you touch the middle icon, you see SMS and MMS messages, and by touching the last icon you see Voicemail (or Visual Voicemail) messages. This Messaging application combines SMS, MMS, and Voicemail in one place, so to follow the steps in this section, touch the middle or SMS/MMS icon.

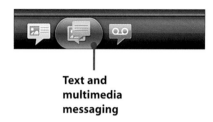

Text and multimedia messaging

2. Touch to reveal all messages in a thread.

3. Touch to search your messages. You can also touch the Search button to perform a search. You can search for anything, such as a word in the texts, name, or phone number.

4. Touch to compose a new SMS or MMS.

5. Touch to change the settings for the Messaging application. See the next section for more information about settings.

6. Touch to delete all message threads.

Number of messages in a thread

Messaging Application Settings

You manage how your SMS and MMS messages are handled through the settings of the Messaging application. Before we actually start working with SMS and MMS, let's take a look at the settings.

1. From the main screen, touch the Menu button and touch Settings.

2. Touch to enable or disable the deletion of messages when their limits per thread are reached. This option works with the options shown in steps 3 and 4.

3. Touch to change the message limit, or the maximum number of text messages, per message thread. The maximum number you can type is 999.

4. Touch to change the message limit, or the maximum number of multimedia messages, per message thread. The maximum number you can type is 999.

5. Touch to enable or disable delivery reports for SMS or text messages that you send.

6. Touch to manage messages stored on your SIM card. This is only valid for GSM Droid models. See more on managing messages on your SIM card in the next section.

7. Touch to enable or disable delivery reports for multimedia messages (MMS).

8. Scroll down to see more options.

It's Not All Good

DELIVERY REPORTS ARE NOT ACCURATE

Currently, if you request a delivery report, you see an icon that shows when a message has been delivered. However, all it is really showing you is that it was successfully sent from your carrier's network, not necessarily if it actually made it to the recipient's phone. Hopefully, this feature will be fixed in a future release of Android.

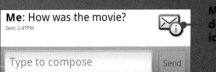

Message delivered icon

9. Touch to enable or disable read reports. This setting depends on many factors including whether the recipient's carrier supports this feature and also whether the recipient allows the return of a read report or read receipt.

10. Touch to enable or disable auto-retrieval of your messages. You probably want to leave this enabled. If you disable this, your messages will not arrive in real-time, which almost defeats the purpose of SMS and MMS.

11. Touch to enable or disable auto-retrieval of your messages when you are roaming on a carrier that is not your own. Because roaming fees can apply, you may choose to leave this disabled.

12. Touch to enable or disable whether a message is displayed in the status bar when new messages arrive.

13. Touch to select the ringtone that plays when you receive new messages.

14. Touch to enable or disable vibration when new messages are received.

Don't Auto Retrieve While Roaming

The reason its best to leave auto-retrieval of messages disabled when you travel to other countries is because auto-retrieving messages when you're roaming can result in a big bill from your provider. International carriers love to charge large amounts of money for people traveling to their country and using their network. The only time it is a good idea to leave this enabled is if your carrier offers an international SMS or MMS bundle where you pay a flat rate upfront before leaving.

Composing Messages

When you compose a new message, you do not need to make a conscious decision whether it will be an SMS (text message) or MMS (multimedia message). As soon as you attach a file to your message, your Droid automatically treats the message as an MMS. Here is how to compose and send messages.

1. Touch to compose a new message.

2. Start typing the phone number of the recipient, or if the person is in your contacts, type the name. If the name is found, touch the mobile number.

3. Touch to start typing your message.

4. Touch to insert a smiley icon.

Touch to select

See the Smiley Icons

To see the actual smiley icons, touch the Menu button and choose Insert Smiley. On some Droids, such as the Droid X, you can only see text versions of the Smiley icons by touching and holding the Smiley icon on the bottom right of the keyboard. The different Smiley faces display and you can choose one.

5. Touch to speak your message.

6. Touch to send your message.

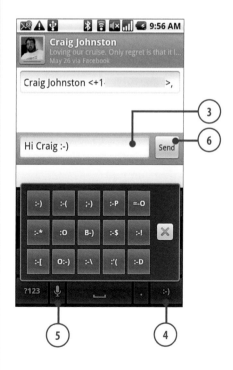

Attaching Files

If you want to send a picture, audio file, or video along with your text message, all you need to do is attach the file. Attaching a file turns your SMS message into an MMS message.

1. After you type your message but before you send your message, touch the Menu button and touch Attach.

2. Touch to attach pictures already stored on your Droid.

3. Touch to take a picture with your Droid's camera and attach it.

4. Touch to attach videos already stored on your Droid.

5. Touch to record a video with your Droid and attach it.

6. Touch to attach audio (music or other audio) already stored on your Droid.

7. Touch to record audio using your Droid and attach it.

8. Touch to attach a picture slideshow if you have previously created one.

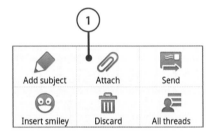

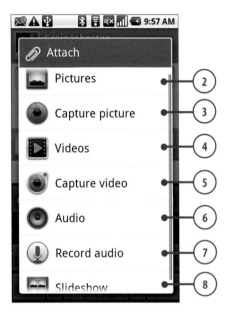

Extra Attachment Types

Some Droids, such as the Droid Incredible, offer two extra types of attachments: Location, which is your current GPS coordinates, and Appointment, which is an existing appointment in your calendar that you can forward to someone.

9. After you have attached one or more files, you see the attachment(s) in the message.

10. Touch to view the attachment full screen instead of as a thumbnail.

11. Touch to replace the attachment with another file.

12. Touch to remove the attachment.

13. Touch to send the message.

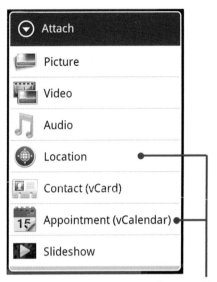

On some Droid models, you can attach GPS coordinates or appointments to messages

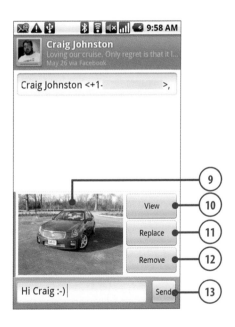

14. If you touch the Back button, your message is instantly saved as a draft message. To continue with the message later, simply touch the message.

Receiving Messages

When you receive a new SMS or MMS, you can read the message, view attachments, and even save the attachments onto your Droid.

1. When a new SMS or MMS arrives you are notified with a ringtone. A notification also displays in the status bar.

2. Pull down the status bar and touch the new message to view it.

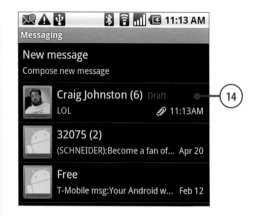

3. Touch the Play icon to view or listen to an attachment.

4. Touch to compose a reply to the message.

5. Touch and hold a message to reveal more options.

6. Touch to prevent a message from being deleted when the thread message limit is reached. Read more about message limits in the "Messaging Application Settings" section earlier in this chapter.

7. Touch to save any attachments to your Droid.

8. Touch to call the sender.

9. Touch to forward the message.

10. Touch to view the message details.

11. Touch to delete the message.

Individual Messages Versus Whole Threads

Using Delete Message in the Message Options deletes only the current message, not the entire message thread. If you want to delete the entire thread of messages, use the Delete Threads option shown in step 6 of the first task in the "Messaging Application" section.

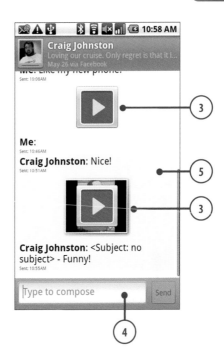

Useable Content

Your Droid is designed to identify phone numbers, web links, and email addresses within messages you create. When it finds them it makes them useable.

1. If there is only one linkable item in the message, you can simply touch the message and your Droid takes the appropriate action. For example, if the message includes one link to a website, the web browser opens and the website loads when you touch the message.

2. If there are multiple linkable items in one message, touch the message to reveal a choice of actions.

3. Touch to send an email to the address listed in the message.

4. Touch to place a call to the number listed in the message.

5. Touch to open the web page listed in the message.

6. Touch Cancel to return to the message screen.

7. Touch and hold the message to see some additional actions.

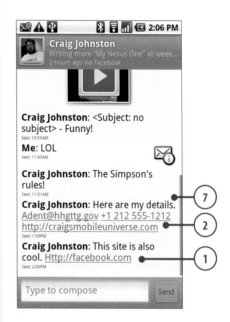

8. Touch to add the email address listed in the message to your Contacts.

9. Touch to add the phone number listed in the message to your Contacts.

In this chapter, you learn how to set the time, use the Clock application, and use the Calendar application. Topics include the following:

→ Synchronizing to the correct time

→ Working with the Clock application

→ Setting alarms

→ Working with the Calendar

Date, Time, and Calendar

With the exception of the Droid X, your Droid has a great Clock application that you can further enhance with the use of the optional Desktop Dock. The Calendar application synchronizes to your Google or Microsoft Exchange Calendars and enables you to create meetings while on the road and to always know where your next meeting is.

Setting the Date and Time

Before we start working with the Clock and Calendar applications, we need to make sure that your Droid has the correct date and time.

1. From the Home screen, touch the Menu button, and touch Settings.

2. Scroll down and touch Date & Time.

3. Touch to enable or disable synchronizing time and date with the wireless carrier. It is best to leave this enabled because it automatically sets date, time, and time zone based on where you are travelling.

4. Touch to set the date if you choose to disable network synchronization.

5. Touch to set the time zone if you choose to disable network synchronization.

6. Touch to set the time if you choose to disable network synchronization.

7. Touch to enable or disable the use of 24-hour time format. This makes your Droid represent time without AM or PM. For example 1:00PM becomes 13:00.

8. Touch to change the way in which the date is represented. For example, in the United States we normally write the date with the month first (12/31/2010). You can make your Droid display the date with day first (31/12/2010), or completely reversed so it displays as 2010/12/31.

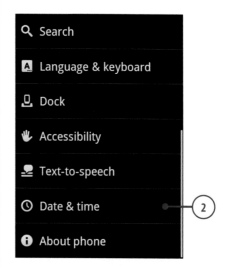

The Clock Application (Droid 1 and 2)

The Clock application is designed to be used as a bedside alarm clock. However unlike a regular alarm clock, the Clock application has some special features. It can display the weather, and it enables you to watch videos or listen to music. The Clock application is very useful, especially when used with the optional Desktop Dock.

Launching the Clock Application

There are two ways to launch the Clock application.

1. Touch the Clock icon from the Home screen. The Droid X does not have a Clock application but you can search the Android Market for an application called DockService, which provides similar functionality.

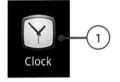

Clock

2. Place your Droid into the Desktop Dock (if available) to automatically launch the Clock application.

>>> Go Further

THE DESKTOP DOCK

When you purchase your Droid, it does not come with the desktop dock. This is something you need to purchase from HTC, Motorola, or another third-party vendor. There are other docks for the Droid, but not all of them utilize the magnets in the Droid for launching the multimedia Dock application or Clock application. The desktop dock has two functions. It charges your Droid, plus it automatically launches the Clock or special Multimedia dock application.

>>> Go Further

FAKE THE DOCK

If for some reason you don't want to purchase a multimedia dock, you can fake it by installing an application called DockService. This makes your Droid think it's resting on a real Dock and launches the multimedia/clock application. Search the Android Market for DockService. You can find some more information about DockService at http://www.appstorehq.com/dock-service-android-276335/app.

Navigating the Clock Application

The Clock application has multiple functions in addition to being a clock, such as operating as an alarm clock, showing the weather, and playing multimedia. The following on-screen buttons are always visible.

1. Touch to return to the Home screen.

2. Touch to play music.

3. Touch to view a slideshow of all pictures stored on your Droid.

4. Touch to manage your alarms.

5. Touch to dim the screen. Touch again to return the screen to its original brightness.

6. Touch to see a 6-day weather report and news.

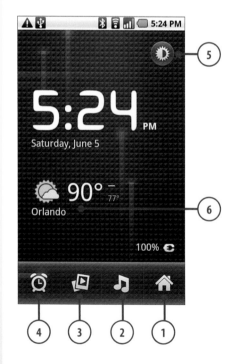

Managing Alarms

The Clock application enables you to set multiple alarms. These can be one-time alarms or recurring alarms. Even if you exit the Clock application, the alarms you set still trigger.

1. Touch to manage your alarms.

2. Touch to add a new alarm.

3. Touch to enable or disable the alarm. The line turns green when an alarm is enabled.

4. Touch to edit the setting for a specific alarm.

5. Touch the Menu button and touch Settings to change the overall alarm settings. See the next section for more on the alarm settings.

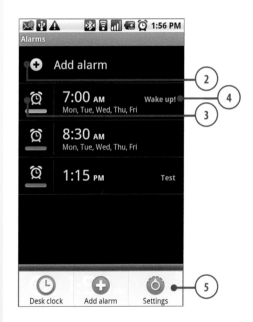

Overall Alarm Settings

Use the Settings button to control
how all alarms function.

1. Touch to enable or disable
   whether to play the alarm even if
   you have your Droid set to Silent
   mode. This is useful at night when
   you don't want to be alerted
   about emails or receive phone
   calls, but you do want your alarm
   to wake you in the morning.

2. Touch to set the alarm volume.

3. Touch to set the duration of the
   snooze period. Your choices range
   between 5 and 30 minutes.

4. Touch to set how the side buttons
   behave if you press any of them
   when the alarm sounds. Your
   choices are Snooze and Dismiss.

Adding and Editing an Alarm

Whether you are adding a new alarm
or editing an existing one, the steps
are the same.

1. Touch Add Alarm or touch a specific alarm to make changes.

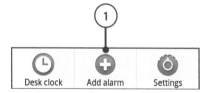

2. Touch to enable or disable the alarm.

3. Touch to set the time the alarm must trigger.

4. Touch to set whether the alarm repeats and on which days of the week. This is useful for setting an alarm that wakes you up only during the week but not on a weekend.

5. Touch to choose the ringtone that plays when the alarm triggers.

6. Touch to enable or disable vibration when the alarm triggers. This is in addition to the ringtone.

7. Touch to add a label for the alarm.

8. Touch Done to save the alarm settings.

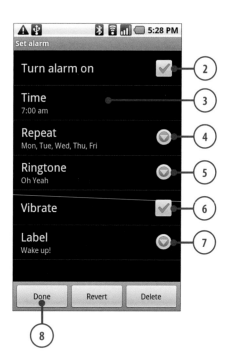

Viewing and Managing Weather and News

If you touch the weather symbol on the Clock main screen, you can view a 6-day weather forecast and read the latest news stories.

1. Touch to switch between the Weather tab and the News tabs. Alternatively, you can swipe your finger from right to left across the Screen to Switch tabs.

2. Touch the Information button to switch to a more detailed view of the weather. Touch it again to return to the 6-day forecast.

3. Touch to manually refresh the weather and news.

4. Touch to change the settings for news and weather.

Modifying the News and Weather Settings

You can modify what city the weather is displayed for, and what kind of news stories you want to read. Start by touching the Settings button on the main weather and news screen.

1. Touch Weather Settings to set whether the weather is displayed based on your GPS location or is for a manually set city. You can also set whether the temperatures are displayed in Celsius or Fahrenheit.

2. Touch News Settings to pick which news topics you want to read and to manage how images are downloaded for each news story. News topics include Top Stories, US, World, Business, Sports, and more.

3. Touch Refresh Settings to set whether your news and weather automatically refresh, and if so, how often.

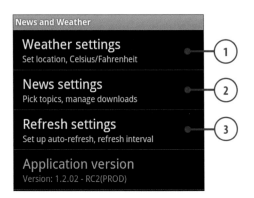

The Clock Application (Droid Incredible and Eris)

The Clock application is designed to be used as a bedside alarm clock. However unlike a regular alarm clock, the Clock application has some special features. It can display the weather, and it has a stopwatch and timer. The Clock application is very useful, especially when used with the optional Desktop Dock.

Launching the Clock Application

There are two ways to launch the Clock application.

1. Touch the Clock icon from the Home screen.

2. Place your Droid into the Desktop Dock (if available) to automatically launch the Clock application.

THE DESKTOP DOCK

>>> Go Further

When you purchase your Droid, it does not come with the desktop dock. This is something you need to purchase from HTC, Motorola, or another third-party vendor. There are other docks for the Droid, but not all of them utilize the magnets in the Droid for launching the multimedia Dock application or Clock application. The desktop dock has two functions. It charges your Droid, plus it automatically launches the Clock or special Multimedia dock application.

Navigating the Clock Application

The Clock application has multiple functions in addition to being a clock, such as operating as an alarm clock, showing the weather, and playing multimedia. The following on-screen buttons are always visible.

1. Touch the Back button to return to the Home screen.

2. Touch to see a 4-day weather report.

3. Touch to dim the screen for night mode. Touch again to return the screen to its regular brightness.

4. Touch to see the world clock.

5. Touch to manage your alarms.

6. Touch to use the stopwatch.

7. Touch to use the timer.

8. Touch to return the clock view.

Managing Alarms

The Clock application enables you to set multiple alarms. These can be one-time alarms or recurring alarms. Even if you exit the Clock application, the alarms you set still triggers.

1. Touch to manage your alarms.

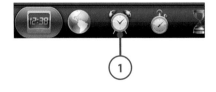

2.   Touch to add a new alarm.

3.   Touch a check mark to enable or disable an alarm. The line turns green when an alarm is enabled.

4.   Touch to edit the setting for a specific alarm.

5.   Touch the Menu button and touch Settings to change the overall alarm settings. See the next section for more on the alarm settings.

6.   Touch the Menu button and touch Delete to delete one or more alarms.

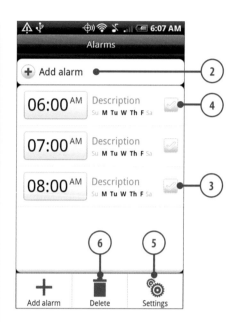

Overall Alarm Settings

Use the Settings button to control how all alarms function.

1.   Touch to enable or disable whether to play the alarm even if you have your Droid set to Silent mode. This is useful at night when you don't want to be alerted about emails or receive phone calls but you do want your alarm to wake you in the morning.

2.   Touch to set the alarm volume.

3.   Touch to set the duration of the snooze period. Your choices range between 5 and 30 minutes.

4.   Touch to set how the side buttons behave if you press any of them when the alarm sounds. Your choices are Snooze and Dismiss.

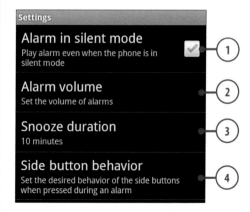

Adding and Editing an Alarm

Whether you are adding a new alarm or editing an existing one, the steps are the same.

1. Touch Add Alarm or touch a specific alarm to make changes.

2. Touch a check mark to enable or disable an alarm.

3. Touch and scroll the hour, minute, and AM/PM wheels to set the time the alarm should trigger.

4. Touch to set whether the alarm repeats and on which days of the week. This is useful for setting an alarm that wakes you up only on weekdays, but not on a weekend.

5. Touch to choose the sound that plays when the alarm triggers.

6. Touch to enable or disable vibration when the alarm triggers. This is in addition to the ringtone.

7. Touch to add a description for the alarm.

8. Touch Done to save the alarm settings.

Viewing and Managing Weather

If you touch the weather symbol on the Clock main screen, you can view a 4-day weather forecast for your current location. You can also add extra cities.

1. Swipe up and down on the screen to switch between the weather at your current location and any extra cities you have added.

2. Touch to manually refresh the weather.

3. Touch to see a more detailed weather forecast for the selected city. This loads the weather details in a web page.

4. Touch to add cities you would for which you'd like to see the weather.

Modifying the Weather Settings

You can modify what city the weather is displayed for, choose Celsius or Fahrenheit and the weather update frequency. Start by touching Menu button on the main weather screen.

1. Touch to rearrange the cities included in the weather application.

2. Touch to manually refresh the weather information.

3. Touch to delete cities.

4. Touch Settings to get to the rest of the weather settings.

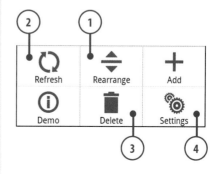

5. Touch to enable or disable automatic weather updates.

6. Touch to change the automatic update frequency.

7. Touch to change from Celsius to Fahrenheit.

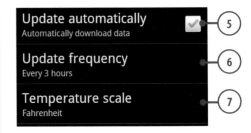

The Calendar Application

The Calendar application enables you to synchronize all of your Google Calendars under your primary Google account to your Droid. You can accept appointments and create and modify appointments right on your phone. Any changes are automatically synchronized wirelessly back to your Google Calendar.

>> Go Further

CALENDAR VIEWS

In the figure of Calendar's main screen, we see the month view. This is where you see the entire month laid out on screen with indicators showing different appointments and where they appear in each day of the month. The week view shows the current week's seven days laid out from left to right. Appointments are visually represented during each day, but because there is more room, you can see the title for each appointment. Day view fills the screen with one day's appointments. Because there is even more room in the Day view, the title and location of each appointment is visible. Agenda view displays your appointments in a list.

The Calendar Main Screen

The main screen of the calendar shows a one-day, one-week, or one-month view of your appointments.

1. Launch the Calendar application.

2. Touch a day's box to view information for that particular day.

3. Touch to view the Agenda.

4. Touch Day to view the calendar one day at a time.

5. Touch Week to view the calendar one week at a time.

6. Touch to add a new event or appointment.

7. Touch to view information on today's calendar.

8. Touch More to see more options including calendar settings and choosing which calendars are displayed.

Indicates an appointment and approximately where in the day it's scheduled

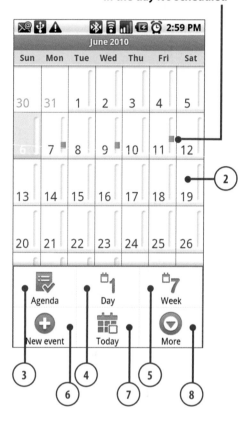

Adding a New Event/Appointment

While you're on the road you can add a new appointment or event and even invite people to it. Events you add synchronize to your Google Calendar in real time. If you have a Droid Incredible or Eris, some of the fields are in different places on the screen.

1. Touch New Event.

Alternative Method to Add an Event

If you touch and hold on a specific hour on a specific day, you see a pop-up window that enables you to create a new event.

2. Touch to enter a title for your event.

3. Touch to select the date the event starts.

4. Touch to enter the time the event starts.

5. Touch to enter the date the event ends.

6. Touch to enter the time the event ends.

7. Touch the All Day check box to make this an all-day event. When you choose to make an all-day event, you can only set the start and end dates, not the start and end times.

8. Enter the location of the event. This can be a full street address.

9. Enter a description for the event. This can include any relevant information about the event, including any conference call numbers, web links, and agenda topics.

10. Scroll down to set more details.

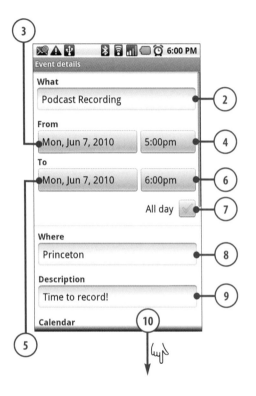

It's Not All Good

ONLY CALENDARS FROM ONE GOOGLE ACCOUNT

The Calendar application synchronizes only with the Google account you used to set up your Droid. Even if you add additional Google accounts in the Gmail application, the Calendar does not synchronize with them. So if you have multiple calendars under your primary Google account you should be okay, but if you use calendars from more than one Gmail account, you will not be able to synchronize those additional calendars.

11. Touch to select which calendar to add the event to. In Google Calendar you might have more than one calendar so that you can keep appointments or events separated. For example, you might have a calendar called Home and one called Work. If your Droid is set up to synchronize with Microsoft Exchange, you can choose that calendar here.

12. Add event attendees. If they are already in your Contacts, their names display. If not, type the attendees' full email addresses. You can add multiple attendees separated by a comma. If your Droid is set up to synchronize with Microsoft Exchange, you should be able to add attendees from your companies address book.

13. Touch the Repetition drop-down to select whether this event repeats.

14. Set how many minutes before the event the reminder will trigger.

15. Add an additional reminder. Additional reminders can be useful to remind yourself or others more than once of an upcoming appointment. For example, you might want to have a reminder the day before an event and a second reminder 30 minutes before the event. You can set up to five reminders in total.

16. Touch the red Minus Sign button next to a reminder to remove that reminder.

17. Touch Done to save the event and return to the calendar main view.

18. Touch Revert to cancel the event creation.

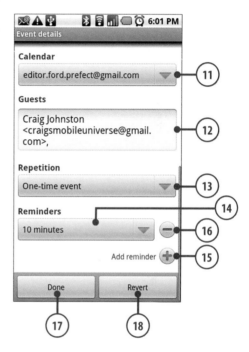

Recurring Events Are Not Flexible

Unfortunately when you choose to make an event repeat, or recur, the choices you are given are not flexible. For example, if you want to set up an event that repeats every Thursday, you cannot do this unless you create the event on a Thursday. Let's hope that this is addressed in a future release of Android.

Editing or Deleting an Event

You can always edit an event that you have created, and sometimes when people invite you to an event, they give you permissions to make changes to it. You can also delete events that you created or that you have been invited to.

1. Touch an event to open it.

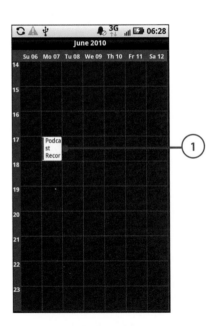

2. Touch the Attending drop-down to change whether you will be attending the event.

3. Touch the Menu button to reveal more options.

4. Touch Add Reminder to add an additional reminder for this event.

5. Touch to edit the event. This option is visible only if you have been given permission to edit the event.

6. Touch to delete the event.

Deleting an Event Automatically Declines It

When you successfully delete an event, the Calendar application sends an event decline notice to the event organizer. So you don't have to first decline the meeting before deleting it because this is all taken care of automatically.

Responding to Event Reminders

If you or the event organizer has set one or more event reminders, you can choose to snooze or dismiss them after they trigger.

1. After you receive an event reminder in the notification bar, pull down the bar and touch the event reminder.

2. Touch to snooze the event reminders for 5 minutes.

3. Touch to dismiss all event reminders.

4. Touch to view the event details.

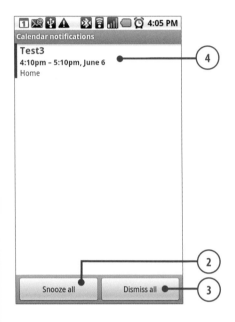

Calendar Settings

You can adjust how the Calendar application behaves and select which calendars you want to synchronize to your Droid.

1. From the Calendar main screen, touch the Menu button and touch More.

2. Touch My Calendars to select which calendars you want to synchronize to your Droid.

3. Touch Settings to modify the calendar settings.

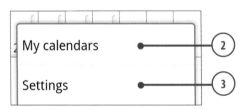

4. Touch Hide Declined Events to enable or disable hiding events that you have declined. You might want to leave them visible in case you change your mind about attending.

5. Touch Set Alerts & Notifications to set how you are alerted when an event reminder triggers. Your choices are Alert, Status Bar Notification, and Off.

6. Touch to select the ringtone that plays when an event reminder triggers.

7. Touch to enable or disable vibration in addition to a visual or audio alert when an event reminder triggers.

8. Touch to set the default reminder time.

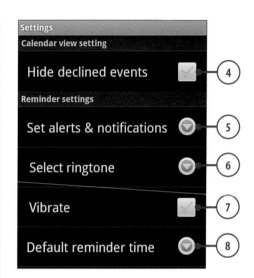

Responding to an Event Invitation

There are actually two ways to respond to an event invitation. You can either respond from your Gmail account or from the Calendar application.

Respond to an Event Invitation in Gmail

When someone invites you to a new event, you receive an email in your Gmail inbox with the details of that meeting.

1. Open the event invitation email in the Gmail application.

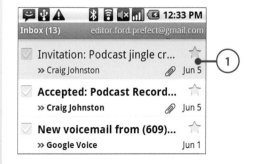

2. Touch Yes, Maybe, or No to indicate whether you will be attending. You might need to use the trackball to make your selection because the links are very close together.

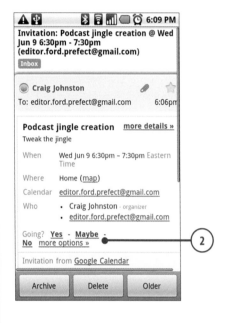

Respond to an Event Invitation in Calendar

When you receive a new event invitation, it is automatically inserted into your calendar even if you have not yet accepted it.

1. Open the Calendar application and look for a new event. Touch the event to open it.

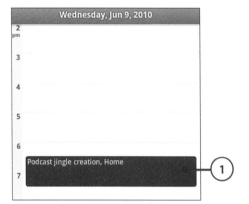

2. Select your response to the event.

In this chapter, you learn how to take pictures with your Droid, how to store them, and how to share them with friends. Topics include the following:

→ Using the camera

→ Sharing pictures

→ Synchronizing pictures

→ Viewing pictures

Taking, Storing, and Viewing Pictures

Your Droid has a decent 5-megapixel camera with mechanical auto-focus. This means it can take really good pictures. After you take those great pictures, you can share them with friends. You can also synchronize the pictures to your computer to possibly print out.

Using the Camera

Let's start by looking at the Camera application before we discuss sharing pictures with friends or synchronizing them with your computer. Remember that you must have a Micro-SD card inserted into your Droid before taking pictures.

How Much Memory Should I Buy?

A 5-megapixel picture is about 1 megabyte in size, on average. If you buy a 2-Gigabyte SD card, you could take about 2,000 pictures with the camera before the card fills up. Of course, you will be using your SD card for everything, music, video, and pictures, so you probably want to buy at least a 4-Gigabyte card or higher.

Original Droid Camera

Let's start with the original Droid's camera.

1. From the Home screen, touch the Camera Application icon to launch the camera. You can also press and hold the Camera button on the right of the Droid until you feel a short vibration that indicates the camera is loading.

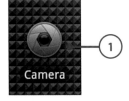

2. Touch to preview your photos in the Gallery application. See more about previewing and working with photos in the Gallery application later in this chapter.

3. Slide the switch up to record video. Slide the switch down to take pictures. Read more about recording video in Chapter 3, "Audio and Video."

4. Touch to take a picture. When you take a picture, your Droid first focuses and then snaps the picture.

The Droid's Physical Camera Button

You can also use the Camera button on the right side of the Droid to take a picture. This button has two positions, halfway pressed and fully pressed. Press the button in gently until you feel it resist. This causes the camera to focus. After it is focused, you hear two beeps. At the same time, a green box appears around the border of the screen. If the box is red, it means you are too close for the camera to focus. If it is green, it means that the camera has focused, and you can take the picture. Press the button in all the way to take the picture.

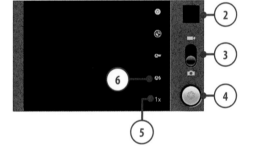

5. Touch to select the zoom level.

6. Touch to change the flash settings. Choose between On, Off, or Automatic. (Your Droid decides when to fire the flash.)

Zooming Is a Waste of Time

Digital zooming is a waste of time. All it does is increase the size of each pixel that makes up your photo. It is not actually zooming. It is a much better practice to simply take pictures at 5 megapixels and then crop the pictures on your computer.

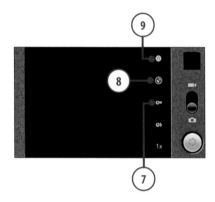

7. Touch to change the white balance settings. Most people leave this on Auto, but you can manually set it for certain lighting conditions such as Incandescent Light, Daylight, Fluorescent Light, or Cloudy Day.

8. Touch to select whether to embed your GPS location in the photo.

What Is the GPS?

GPS stands for Global Positioning System. Your Droid has a built-in Assisted GPS (A-GPS) chip that calculates where you are on planet Earth. If you choose to, when you take a picture, your Droid embeds the GPS coordinates in the picture, so if you use an Apple Mac with iPhoto, you can see where you were when you took the picture. Some photo websites such as Flickr offer the same feature.

9. Touch to change the focus mode and exposure settings. Change the focus settings from Auto to Infinity or Macro. Macro is used for objects that are close up.

Using the Infinity Option

Choosing Infinity for the Focus Mode disables the auto-focus and sets the focus to Infinity, which means that pictures can be snapped more quickly, but you cannot take pictures of close objects.

Droid Incredible and Droid Eris Camera

The HTC Droid Incredible and Droid Eris share the same camera application. Let's take a look at it.

1. From the Home screen, touch the Camera application icon to launch the camera.

2. Touch to change the camera settings.

3. Touch to change the flash mode from automatic to always on or always off.

4. Touch to change the zoom level.

5. Touch to review, share, and delete pictures in the Photos application. See more about the Photos application later in this chapter.

6. Touch to focus on an area of the picture.

7. Touch and hold to focus on an area of the picture and take the picture.

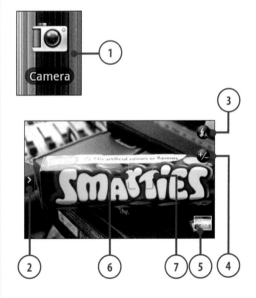

Focus on Parts of a Picture

With the Droid Incredible camera, you can actually focus on a certain part of a picture. By touching the part of the picture you want in focus, you will see that the rest of the picture goes out of focus. Using this trick allows you to take some amazing pictures.

Camera Settings

When you touch the camera settings arrow, you can change all the camera settings and even make use of effects.

1. Touch to change the camera mode from Photo (still pictures) to Video.

2. Touch to change the exposure level of the pictures. This equates to the brightness of the pictures because exposing them for more or less time than normal affects how bright or dim they are.

3. Touch to change the image properties of each picture, such as contrast, color saturation, and sharpness.

Brighter

Darker

4. Touch to add effects to pictures, such as gray scale, sepia (old photo look), and negative (colors are reversed).

5. Touch to adjust more camera settings, such as white balance, ISO, resolution, and more.

Droid X Camera

The Droid X has its own camera application that does not share any similarities with the two Droids described in the previous sections. Let's take a tour of the Droid X camera.

1. Touch to launch the Camera.

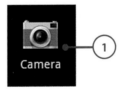

Camera

2. This is the current location calculated by the GPS chip.

3. Touch to review pictures in the Gallery application. See more about reviewing, sharing, and editing pictures in the Gallery application for the Droid X later in this chapter.

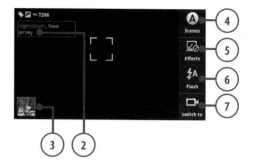

4. Touch to select different scenes for your picture. Scenes are predefined camera settings that configure it for situations such as night portrait, sports, and more.

5. Touch to add effects such as negative, sepia, black and white to your pictures.

6. Touch to change the flash mode from automatic to always on or always off.

7. Touch to switch between photo and video mode.

8. Press the physical Camera button in halfway until you hear two beeps. If the block in the center of the screen turns red, then the Droid camera was not able to focus. If it turns green, it means it is able to focus. Press the camera button in all the way to snap the picture.

Camera Modes

The Droid X camera can be set to certain modes such as Single Shot (that's normal mode), Panorama Assist, Self-portrait, and Multi-shot. Let's take a look at each one. To get to these camera modes, follow these steps.

1. Touch the Menu button while in the main camera view and then touch Picture Modes.

2. Touch Panorama Assist. This mode helps you take panoramic photos by guiding you from one shot to the next. Each panorama consists of six pictures that are stitched together to make one photo. Each picture in the panorama is 3 megapixels.

3. Choose which type of panoramic picture you want to take. In this example we choose Move Right, which means we start on the left of a scene and move progressively to the right.

4. Take the first picture in the panorama. You then see a guide appear at the bottom left of the screen. Move the Droid slowly to the right. You see the camera thumbnail moving to the right into the next panorama position. As it gets into the box, the camera automatically takes the next picture.

5. Continue moving to the right until the camera takes six pictures. After the sixth picture, the camera automatically stitches the pictures together to form one large panoramic photo.

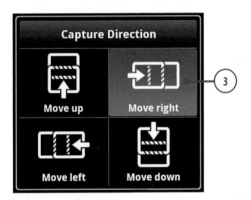

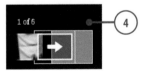

>>> Go Further

TAKE YOUR OWN PORTRAIT

Your Droid can use its face recognition technology to take perfect portrait pictures of yourself.

Touch the Menu button and then touch Picture Modes. Touch Self Portrait. Turn the Droid around so the camera is facing you. You do not need to press the physical Camera button. Try to aim the camera at your face. When your Droid detects a face, it takes the picture automatically.

If your Droid cannot detect a face, you see a message on the screen informing you of this.

>>> Go Further

TAKE PICTURES IN SPURTS

Your Droid can snap six pictures instead of one when you press the Camera button. The only drawback is that each picture is only 1 megapixel, but it does allow you to potentially get the right shot.

Touch the Menu button and then touch Picture Modes. Touch Multi-shot. Take a picture as you normally would by pressing the Camera button. Your Droid takes six pictures in quick succession.

Picture Tags

When you take pictures on your Droid X, it can embed tags in the pictures. Normally it will embed the GPS coordinates and place names in the pictures, but you can add your own tags, especially if you know that GPS is not locking in.

1. Touch the Menu button while in the main camera view and then touch Tags.

2. Touch to disable or enable auto location tagging. Location tagging uses GPS to calculate where you are.

3. Touch to enable or disable custom tags.

4. Touch to add custom tags.

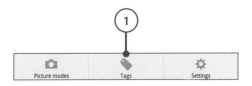

Camera Settings

Using camera settings you can change things such as the resolution of each picture, picture review time, and more. Let's take a look.

1. Touch the Menu button while in the main camera view and then touch Settings.

2. Touch to change the picture resolution.

3. Touch to change the video resolution. Read more about video in Chapter 3.

4. Touch to set up the album to which photos are uploaded when you choose Quick Upload chosen. This can be Facebook, MySpace, Photobucket, Picasa, or a specific email address.

5. Touch to change the picture review time. This is how long the picture remains on the screen after you take it.

6. Scroll down to see more options.

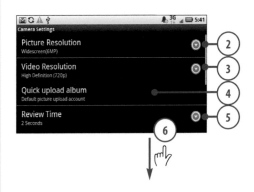

7. Touch to enable or disable face recognition.

8. Touch to change the ISO settings.

9. Touch to change the Exposure setting.

10. Touch to enable or disable the shutter animation from None to Circle or Curtain. The shutter animation simply simulates an old nondigital camera's lens shutter. It serves no purpose other than to look cool.

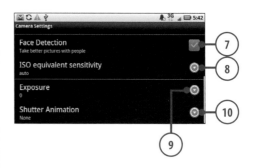

Viewing and Managing Your Photos

No matter if you have snapped pictures using your Droid, or have synchronized photos from a computer, you can use the Gallery application (original Droid, Droid 2, and Droid X) or the Photos application (Droid Eris and Incredible) to manage, edit, and share your photos.

Gallery (Droid and Droid 2)

The Gallery application on the Droid and Droid 2 is different from the one on the Droid X. Let's take a look at it.

1. Touch to launch the Gallery application.

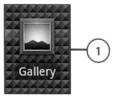

2. Touch a thumbnail photo to open an album. Touch and hold on an album to reveal the album menu.

3. Touch the Camera icon to launch the Camera application.

4. Touch and drag your finger on the screen to see all photo albums.

5. Touch the photos labeled as Camera to see pictures taken on your Droid.

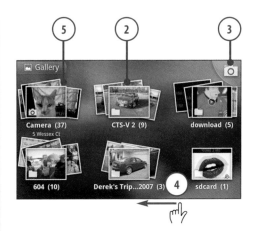

The Tilt Trick

While on the main Gallery screen, to see photos lower in the album stack, tilt your Droid forward and backward or side to side. As you tilt, you notice that the view tilts with you, allowing you to see more of the photos that are lower in the stack.

Album Menu

When you touch and hold on an album, the album menu appears. The menu enables you to share the album, delete it, or see its details.

1. Touch to share the photo album. You can share the album on Picasa, or send it via Bluetooth, Gmail, Email, or MMS.

2. Touch to delete the photo album.

3. Touch to see the photo's filename.

4. Touch to select all photo albums.

5. Touch to deselect all photo albums.

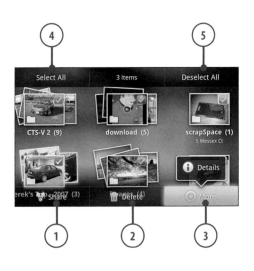

No Facebook Album Sharing
Strangely, you cannot share a photo album on Facebook. You can share photos with Picasa, though. Let's hope that a future version of Android will allow sharing with Facebook.

Managing and Sharing Photos in an Album

After you open a photo album, you can manage the photos in it, edit them, and share them.

1. Touch an album to see all pictures in it.

2. Slide to switch between stacked and grid views.

3. Slide left and right to rapidly move through the pictures.

4. Touch a picture to open it.

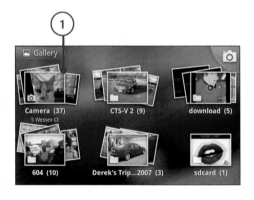

Touch this to return to the main Gallery screen

The name of the album you are viewing

Review, Edit, and Share Pictures

After you open a picture you can review it, edit it, and share it.

1. Touch the picture to reveal the menus.

2. Touch to launch the camera.

3. Touch to view a slideshow of all pictures in the album.

4. Touch to zoom in and out.

5. Swipe left and right to scroll between the pictures in the album.

6. Touch to see more options such as sharing pictures, cropping them, and using them as wallpaper.

Sharing Your Pictures

If you touch the More button while you're looking at a photo in the picture review screen (step 6 in the "Reviewing Pictures" section), you can share your pictures.

1. Touch to share your picture.

2. Touch to email the picture via Gmail.

3. Touch to upload the picture to Facebook.

4. Touch to upload the picture to Twitter.

5. Touch to send the picture via MMS.

6. Touch to send the picture to another device via Bluetooth.

7. Touch to upload the picture to the Picasa photo site.

8. Touch to use the Google Goggles service to figure out what is in the picture.

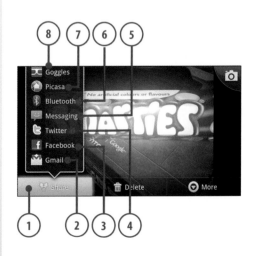

What Is Goggles?

Google Goggles is a service that analyzes pictures you take on your Smartphone and tries to determine what it "sees" in the picture. It is quite accurate at doing this. After Goggles figures it out, it shows you more information on the object it "sees" and where you can buy it. You can read more about Google Goggles at http://www.google.com/mobile/goggles/#text.

Rotating, Cropping, and Mapping Pictures

If you touch the More button while you're looking at a photo in the picture review screen (step 6 in the "Reviewing Pictures" section), you can crop the picture, rotate it, and see it on a map.

1. Touch to rotate the picture right.

2. Touch to rotate the picture left.

3. Touch to see the details about the picture, such as the size of it on the memory card, the filename, the date it was taken, and the album it is in. The details might include META data such as the GPS coordinates if they were originally inserted.

4. Touch Show on Map to see where you were standing when you took the picture. You have a choice of whether to plot the location using Google Maps on the Internet or using the Google Maps application on your Droid.

5. Touch to crop the picture.

6. Touch to set the picture as your wallpaper or Contact icon.

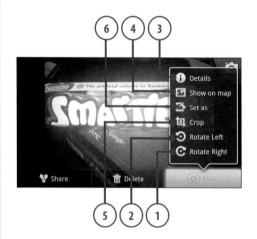

It's Not All Good

CANNOT CREATE AN ALBUM

Although you can edit, delete, and share a photo album (as described in the "Album Menu" section), you cannot create a new album. The only way to create a new photo album is on your desktop computer and synchronize it to your Droid.

Photos (Droid Incredible and Eris)

The Droid Incredible and Droid Eris use the Photos application and do not have the Gallery application installed. Here is how to manage your photos in the Photos application.

1. Touch to launch Photos.

2. Touch to see your Facebook photo albums and those of your friends on Facebook.

3. Touch to see photo albums on Flickr.

4. Touch to see photo albums on your Droid.

5. Touch an album to see the album view.

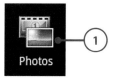

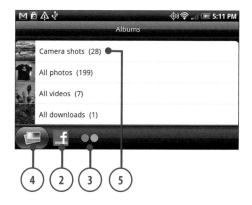

Review, Edit, and Share Pictures in Album View

When you open the album view, you can review, edit, and share pictures.

1. Touch an album in the main Photos screen to see the pictures in the album.

2. Touch to return to the camera.

3. Touch to select one or more pictures to delete.

4. Touch to share the picture with people via Bluetooth, Facebook, Flickr, Gmail, MMS, Peep, or Picasa. See more about sharing pictures later in this chapter.

5. Touch to see all photo albums.

6. Touch a picture to see it full screen.

7. Swipe left and right to scroll between the pictures.

8. Touch a picture to make it full screen, and touch the Menu button to see more choices.

9. Touch to view a slideshow of the pictures.

10. Touch to share the picture. See more about sharing pictures later in this chapter.

11. Touch to set the picture as a contact icon, favorite, footprint, or wallpaper.

12. Touch to rotate the picture.

13. Touch to select one or more pictures to delete.

14. Touch to see more choices such as cropping the picture.

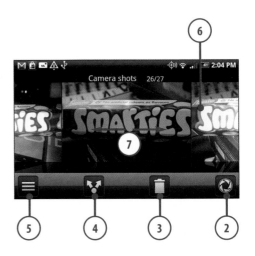

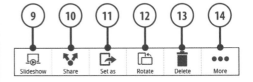

15. Touch to crop the picture. See more about cropping your pictures below.

16. Touch to see details about the picture.

17. Touch to change the album settings. See more about album settings in the later in the chapter.

Sharing Your Pictures

If you touch the Share button while you're looking at a photo in the picture review screen (step 8 in the "Reviewing Pictures" section), you can share your pictures.

1. Touch to share on Facebook using the HTC Sense interface. This choice offers the ability upload multiple pictures and add captions to each. You can also share on Facebook without using the HTC Sense interface by touching the Facebook option at the top of the list.

2. Touch to upload the picture to Flickr. (You need a Flickr account to use this option.)

3. Touch to send the picture to someone via Gmail.

4. Touch to send the picture to someone via the Mail client (non-Gmail).

5. Touch to send the picture to someone using MMS.

6. Touch to upload the picture Twitter using Peep. Peep is a Twitter client included on the Droid Incredible and Eris.

7. Touch to share the picture on Picasa. Because Picasa belongs to Google, you do not need a separate account.

Cropping Pictures

If you touch the More button while you're looking at a photo in the picture review screen (step 13 in the "Reviewing Pictures" section), you can crop the picture.

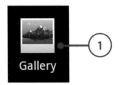

1. Touch and move the green crop box to adjust where the picture should be cropped.

2. Touch to save the picture. The new version overwrites your original, so make sure you're happy with the picture before you touch Save.

3. Touch to cancel the crop and leave the picture as is.

Gallery (Droid X)

Although the Droid 1 and 2 share the same Gallery application with the Droid X, the version of the application on the Droid X is very different. Let's take a look.

1. Touch to launch the Gallery application.

2. The main Gallery view shows all photo albums. This includes the Camera Roll album that includes all pictures taken with the Droid X's camera.

3. Touch the Menu button to see an option to launch the camera and go to the Gallery application settings.

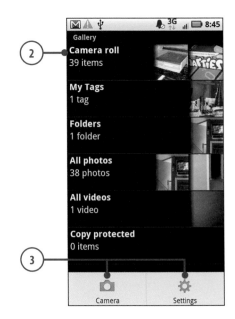

Settings

The Gallery application has a few settings such as the slideshow interval, slideshow transition, and more. Let's take a look.

1. Touch to change the slideshow interval to 2, 3, or 4 seconds.

2. Touch to enable or disable slide show repetition.

3. Touch to enable or disable slide shuffling.

4. Touch to change the slideshow transitions to fade, slide left, swing, or forward.

5. Touch to set the quick upload album. This is the place that photos are sent when you choose the Quick Upload option.

6. Touch to enable or disable auto-completing tags that match contact names.

Reviewing, Sharing, and Editing Pictures

When you touch an album, you see all pictures in that album. From there you can share them, edit them, or simply view them. Let's take a look.

1. Touch to view a picture.

2. Touch to play a video.

3. Touch to launch the camera.

4. Touch to start a slideshow of all pictures in the current album.

5. Touch to jump to a specific date range. This can be today, last week, this month, or last month.

6. Touch to select multiple items. This enables you to select multiple items and then touch the Menu button to share them, tag them, delete them, or print them.

7. Touch to go to the Gallery settings. See the "Settings" section earlier in this chapter for more information.

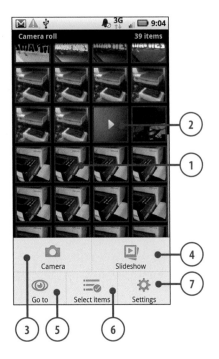

Reviewing and Sharing Pictures

When you touch a picture in an album you can view it, edit it, share it, and even print it. Let's see how.

1. Touch a picture in an album to view it full screen, and then touch the Menu button to reveal extra options.

2. Touch to launch the camera.

3. Touch to do a quick upload. This enables you to upload the picture to a predetermined location such as an email address, Facebook, or Picasa.

4. Touch to share the picture via Bluetooth, Gmail, Picasa, or MMS.

5. Touch to edit the picture.

6. Touch to delete the picture.

7. Touch to see more options such as setting the picture as your wallpaper or contact picture and printing the picture at a local store.

Editing Pictures

When you edit a picture, you can add tags to it, rotate it, add effects, and even add text to it. Touch the Menu button and touch Edit to see the Edit menu.

1. Touch to add tags to the picture.

2. Touch to rotate the picture.

3. Touch for more advanced editing features.

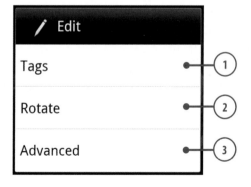

4. Touch to change brightness and contrast of the picture.

5. Touch to adjust color and color saturation of the picture.

6. Touch to add effects to the picture.

7. Touch to resize the picture.

8. Touch to crop the picture.

9. Touch to add text and text bubbles to the picture.

10. Touch to add clip art to the picture.

11. Scroll down to see more options.

12. Touch to add stamps to the picture.

13. Touch to add frames around the picture.

14. Touch to flip the picture.

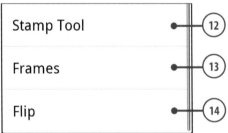

Printing Pictures

The Gallery application enables you to print pictures to a printer that supports Bluetooth or to send them to a local store near you that can print them for you. While you're viewing a picture you want to print, touch the Menu button and then touch More.

1. Touch Print.

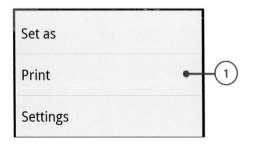

2. Touch to print the picture to a printer that supports Bluetooth. Before you can use this feature, you must have already paired your Droid X with the Printer. Please see Chapter 4, "Connecting to Bluetooth, Wi-Fi, and VPNs," for more information on Bluetooth.

3. Touch to print the picture to a local store.

4. Your Droid X uses GPS to look for local retailers that support this feature. After it has found some, touch a retailer to send the picture to it.

When to Use City and ZIP

If you do not want to rely on your Droid X to find a place to print your photos, or you don't want to pick a local place for any reason, you can touch Search by City or ZIP Code to bypass your location completely.

Synchronizing Photos with Your Computer

When you connect your Droid to a computer, you can move pictures back and forth manually, or by using software like The Missing Sync or doubleTwist. In this section we cover how to synchronize manually and how to do it using doubleTwist. If you have not yet installed doubleTwist, follow the installation steps in the Prologue.

Manually Working with Pictures

The most generic way of working with photos and photo albums is to mount your Droid as a drive on your computer.

1. Plug your Droid into your computer using the supplied USB cable.

2. Pull down the status bar to reveal the USB Connected notification.

3. Touch the USB Connected notification.

4. Touch Turn on USB Storage, and your Droid's external memory (the Micro-SD card) is mounted as a drive on your computer. If you have a Mac, the drive is called DROID, NO NAME or Untitled 1. If you have Windows, the drive is called Removable Disk (X:).

Alternative Names for USB Drive

If you have a Motorola Droid X, HTC Droid Incredible, or HTC Droid Eris, when you touch the USB Connected notification, you see a different screen than the one shown for the Motorola Droid. To select USB Storage on the Droid X, touch USB Mass Storage. To select USB Storage on the Incredible and Eris, touch Disk Drive.

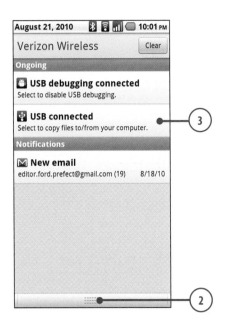

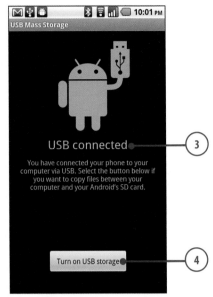

Moving Pictures (Mac OSX)

After your Droid is connected to your Mac and mounted, you can browse the Droid just like any other drive on your computer. The pictures are in a folder called DCIM.

1. Browse to your Droid to locate the pictures.

Where Are the Pictures?
Pictures taken with the Droid's camera are in DCIM\Camera. All other pictures are in a folder called Images.

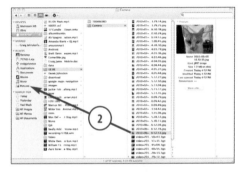

2. Drag one or more pictures from your Droid to a folder on your Mac.

3. When you are done, remember to right-click on the drive and choose Eject. This is crucial to preserving the contents of your Droid.

Moving Pictures (Windows)

After your Droid is connected to your Windows computer and mounted, you can browse the Droid just like any other drive on your computer. The pictures are in a folder called DCIM.

1. When the AutoPlay window appears, click Open Folder to View Files.

Where Are the Pictures?

Pictures taken with the Droid's camera are in DCIM\Camera. All other pictures are in a folder called Images.

2. Drag one or more pictures from your Droid to a folder on your Windows computer.

3. When you are done, remember to right-click on the drive and choose Eject. This is crucial to pre-serving the contents of your Droid.

Creating Photo Albums

There is currently no way to cre-ate photo albums on your Droid or in doubleTwist. To manually create photo albums, browse your Droid after it is connected to a computer. Create a new folder called Images, if it doesn't already exist. Under the folder Images, create a new folder for each new photo album you want to create. The name of the folder becomes the name of the photo album. Copy photos to your new folders. After you eject the Droid, your new photo albums are visible in the Gallery application.

Automated Picture Importing (Mac OSX)

When you mount your Droid as a drive on a Mac, iPhoto normally launches. This is because iPhoto sees the Droid as a digital camera.

1. Click on the camera named NO NAME. This is your Droid.

2. Enter details of the pictures.

3. Click Import All.

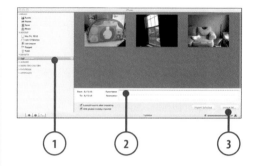

Automated Picture Importing (Windows)

When you mount your Droid as a drive on a Windows computer, the AutoPlay window always appears.

1. Click Import Pictures.

2. Enter one or more tags for the pictures. A tag is a key word.

3. Click Import.

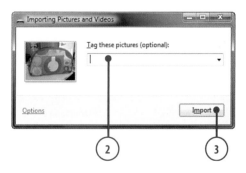

Working with doubleTwist

doubleTwist is a free download that enables you to synchronize media to and from your Droid. If you have not yet installed doubleTwist, follow the instructions in the Prologue. The steps described here are the same for Windows and Mac OSX.

1. Connect and mount your Droid so that it displays under Devices in doubleTwist.

2. Click Photos.

3. Drag one or more pictures from your Droid to the Photos folder in the doubleTwist Library. Your pictures are physically stored on your computer in a folder called doubleTwist, which is within the Pictures folder.

4. Click to send one or more pictures to Facebook.

5. Click to send one or more pictures to Flickr.

6. Click Send to email one or more pictures.

7. To copy pictures from your doubleTwist library to your Droid, click on Photos and drag one or more pictures to Photos on your Droid.

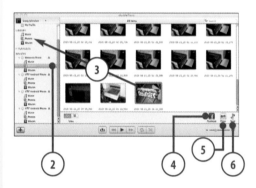

Configure doubleTwist Photo Options (Mac OSX)

Your doubleTwist Photo Library can be configured to show one or more folders on your computer where you normally store pictures. On a Mac, your iPhoto library is automatically a part of the doubleTwist library.

1. Click doubleTwist, Preferences.

2. Click Library.

3. Click to add new folders.

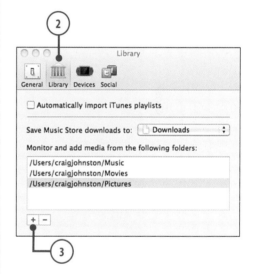

Configure doubleTwist Photo Options (Windows)

Your doubleTwist Photo Library can be configured to show one or more folders on your computer where you normally store pictures.

1. Click Edit, Preferences.

2. Select the Library tab.

3. Click a Folder button to add new folders.

4. Click to save.

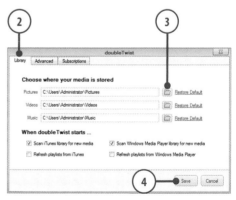

In this chapter, you learn how to purchase and use Android applications on your Droid. Topics include the following:

- → Finding applications with Android Market
- → Purchasing applications
- → Keeping applications up to date
- → Killing applications

Working with Android Applications

Your Droid comes with enough applications to make it a worthy Smartphone. However, wouldn't it be great to play games, update your Facebook and Twitter statuses, or even keep a grocery list? Well, finding these types of applications is what the Android Market is for, and we explore it in this chapter.

Configuring Google Checkout

Before you start buying applications in the Android Market, you must first sign up for a Google Checkout account. If you plan to download only free applications, you do not need a Google Checkout account.

1. From a desktop computer or your Droid, open the web browser and go to http://checkout.google.com.

2. Sign in using the Google account that you used to set up your Droid.

3. Choose your location. If your country is not listed, you have to use free applications until it's added to the list.

4. Enter your credit card number. This can also be a debit card that includes a Visa or MasterCard logo, also known as a check card, so that the funds actually are withdrawn from your checking account.

5. Select the month and year of the card's expiration date.

6. Enter the card's CVC number, which is also known as the security code. This is a three- or four-digit number that's printed on the back of your card.

7. Enter your name.

8. Enter your billing address.

9. Enter your phone number.

10. Although you don't need a mailing address for the Android Market, you might want to choose an alternative delivery address for items your purchase from online stores that use Google Checkout.

11. Click Create My Account when you're done with the form.

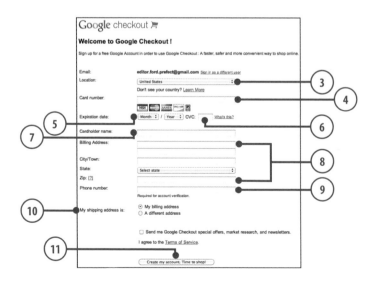

Navigating Android Market

Android is the operating system that runs your Droid and, therefore, any applications that are made for your Droid need to run on Android. The Android Market is a place where you can search for and buy Android applications.

1. From the Home screen, touch the Market application icon.

2. Touch the Search button to search the entire Market.

3. Touch Apps to browse all non-game applications.

4. Touch Games to browse only games.

5. Touch Downloads to see applications that you have previously downloaded.

6. Touch an application to see more about it. You can either touch an application that's featured at the top of the screen, or you can touch one that's listed at the bottom of the screen.

7. Press the Menu button to reveal additional options.

8. Touch to search for applications.

9. Touch to see applications that you have previously downloaded.

10. Touch for help using Android Market.

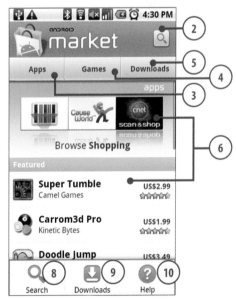

Browsing Apps by Category

If you know the type of application you want to buy or download, but want to see what is available, you can browse by category. The following steps work the same for games or other applications.

1. Touch either Apps or Games.

2. Touch a category or All Games.

3. Touch to see the top paid applications. This is a list of top applications that are not free.

4. Touch to see the top free applications. This is a list of top applications that are free.

5. Touch to see what applications have just been added to the Android Market.

6. Touch an application to buy or download it, if it is free.

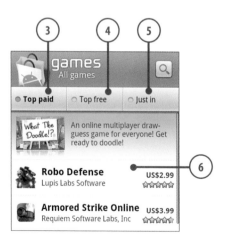

Downloading Free Applications

You don't have to spend money to get quality applications. Some of the best applications are actually free.

1. Browse through the applications and touch the application you want to download.

2. Scroll down to read the application features, reviews by other people who installed it, and information on the person or company who wrote the application.

3. Touch Install to download and install the application.

4. While the application downloads, you see the download icon on the notification bar.

Buying Applications

If an application is not free, the price is displayed next to the application icon. If you want to buy the application, remember that you need to already have a Google Checkout account. See the "Configuring Google Checkout" section earlier in the chapter for more information.

1. Touch the application you want to buy.

What If the Currency Is Different?

When you browse applications in the Android Market, you might see applications that have prices in foreign currencies. In our example, the price is in euros. When you purchase an application, the currency is simply converted into your local currency using the exchange rate at the time of purchase.

2. Scroll down to read the application features, reviews by other people who installed it, and information on the person or company who wrote the application.

3. Touch to buy the application.

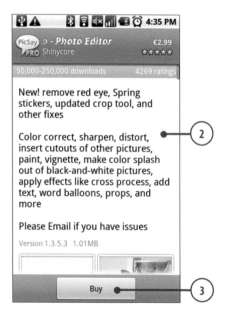

4. Read the notices about what information this application wants to access on your Droid. Pay attention to this information as you might not want an application having access to something on your phone.

5. Touch OK to agree to allow the application to access your information. If you don't agree, touch Cancel.

6. On the payment screen, if you have not yet set up your Google Checkout account, touch the payment method drop-down list.

7. Choose either to bill your carrier account or to use a credit card. Billing your wireless carrier might not be available on Verizon in the United States.

8. Touch Buy Now to download and install the application.

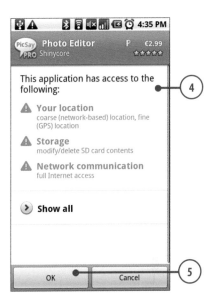

Deleting Applications

If you no longer have a need for a specific application, you can delete it from your Droid. There are actually two ways of doing this.

Deleting an Application Using Settings

One way you can delete applications is to use the Settings menu. Using this method you can delete any application regardless of whether it was downloaded via the Market application or preinstalled on your Droid.

1. From the Home screen, press the Menu button and touch Settings.

2. Touch Applications.

3. Touch Manage Applications.

4. Touch the Menu button to reveal the menu.

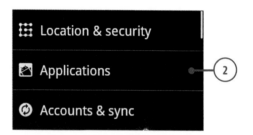

5. Touch to sort the applications by their size, which you might want to do if you are looking to increase available memory on your Droid and need to find large applications to delete.

6. Touch to change the filter. You can filter by applications that are currently running, applications that have been downloaded, or all applications.

7. Touch the application you want to delete.

8. Touch Uninstall.

9. Touch OK to uninstall the application.

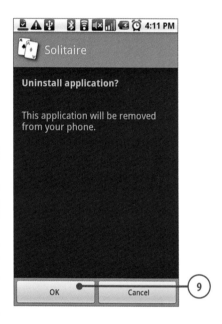

Deleting an Application Using Market

The other way to delete applications is by using the Market application. With this method, you can delete only applications that you have downloaded using the Market application.

1. From the Home screen, launch the Market application.

2. From the Market application's main screen, touch the Menu button and touch Downloads.

3. Touch the application that you want to delete.

4. Touch Uninstall.

5. Touch OK when the warning message is displayed.

Accidentally Uninstall an Application?

What if you accidentally uninstall an application, or you uninstalled an application in the past but now decide you'd like to use it again? To get the application back, go to the Downloads view in Android Market. Scroll to that application and touch it. Touch Install to reinstall it.

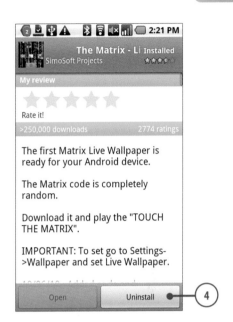

6. Select a reason why you are removing the application, or choose I'd Rather Not Say.

7. Touch OK to uninstall the application.

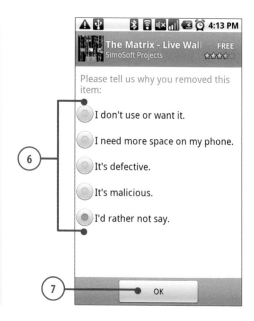

Keeping Applications Up to Date

Developers who write Android applications often update their applications to fix bugs or to add new features. With a few quick touches it is easy for you to update the applications that you have installed.

1. If an application you have installed has an update, you see the update notification in the notification bar.

2. Pull down the notification bar and touch on the update notification.

3. The Android Market application loads and switches to the Download screen.

4. A list of all applications you have downloaded displays. The applications that have updates available are designated with the orange Update Available note.

5. Touch one of the applications that has an update available.

6. Touch Update.

7. Touch OK when the warning screen appears.

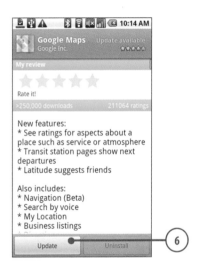

8. Touch OK to download and install the application update.

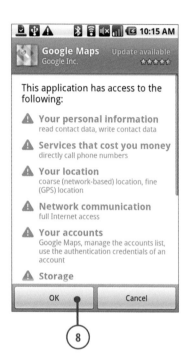

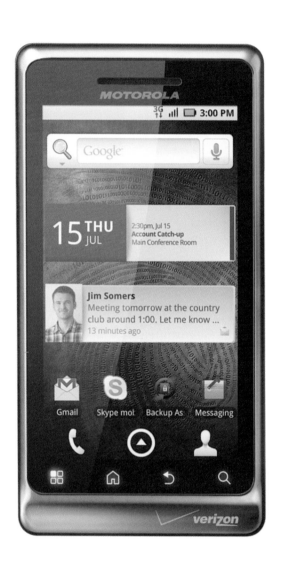

In this chapter, you learn how to customize your Droid to suit your needs and lifestyle. Topics include the following:.

→ Changing wallpapers and live wallpapers
→ Using Scenes
→ Replacing the keyboard
→ Changing sound and display settings
→ Setting region and language

Customizing Your Droid

Your Droid arrives preconfigured to appeal to most buyers; however, you might want to change the way some of the features work or even personalize it to fit your mood or lifestyle. Luckily your Droid is customizable.

Changing Your Wallpaper

Your Droid comes preloaded with a cool live wallpaper that animates. You can install other live wallpapers, use static wallpapers, and even use pictures in the Gallery application as your wallpaper. We start by selecting a static wallpaper.

1. Touch the Menu button while on the Home screen.

2. Touch Wallpaper.

3. Touch Wallpapers.

4. Touch a wallpaper to select and view it.

5. Touch Set Wallpaper after you have found a wallpaper you like. After you touch Set Wallpaper, the wallpaper is changed and you are returned to the Home screen.

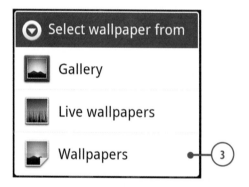

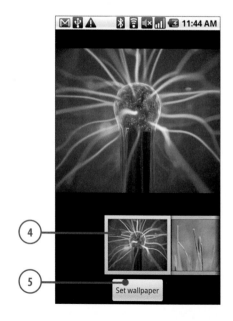

Wallpaper from Gallery Pictures

Instead of using specific wallpaper images, you can choose pictures from your Gallery to use as your Droid's wallpaper.

1. Touch the Menu button while on your Home screen.

2. Touch Wallpaper.

3. Touch Gallery.

4. Touch to use your Droid's camera to take a picture and use it as your wallpaper.

5. Touch to open your Gallery and find a picture you want to use as wallpaper. Touch the photo to select it.

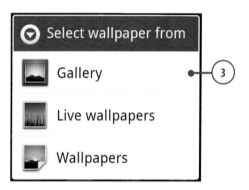

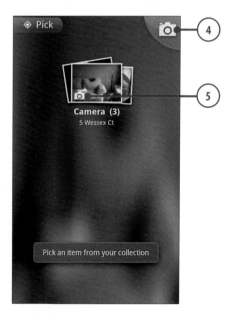

6. Use the cropping box to adjust the way the picture is cropped before you use it as a wallpaper. Remember to expand the cropping box to the full picture size if you want to use the whole picture.

7. Touch to discard any changes and return to the Gallery to choose another picture.

8. Touch Save to use the picture as your wallpaper.

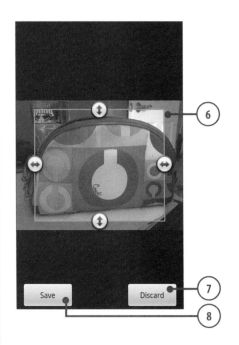

Live Wallpaper

Live wallpaper is wallpaper with some intelligence behind it. It can be a cool animation, or even an animation that keys off things like the music you are playing on your Droid, or it can be something simple such as the time. There are some very cool live wallpapers, including one that plays the game Pong to keep the time.

1. Touch the Menu button while on your Home screen.

2. Touch Wallpaper.

3. Touch Live Wallpapers.

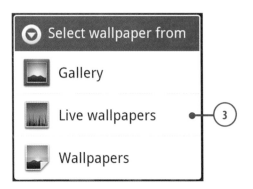

4. Touch a live wallpaper that you want to use.

5. A preview of the live wallpaper is displayed.

6. Touch Settings to review and change the settings for the current live wallpaper. The settings you see on this screen are specific to the Live Wallpaper you have chosen.

7. Touch Set Wallpaper to use the live wallpaper.

Find More Wallpaper

You can find wallpaper or live wallpaper in the Android Market. Open Market and search for "wallpaper" or "live wallpaper." Read more on how to use the Android Market in Chapter 10, "Working with Android Applications."

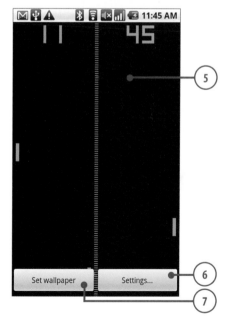

Using Scenes (HTC Droids Only)

If you have a Droid made by HTC, such as the HTC Droid Incredible or HTC Droid Eris, it comes preloaded with something called Scenes. Scenes are similar to Themes on other Smartphones and Windows computers. They change the wallpaper and add widgets to the different Home screens on your Droid. The idea is that you can switch Scenes depending on your mood. You can use a Work Scene while at work and then switch it to a Play Scene after hours.

Changing the Scene

Depending on your mood, you might want to choose a new Scene that changes the style and Home screen layout. Here is how.

1. Touch the Menu button while on the Home screen and then touch Scenes.

2. Touch the Scene that you want to switch to.

3. Touch Done to see the Home screen that now has the Scene applied and looks completely different.

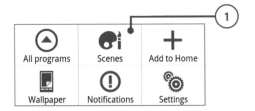

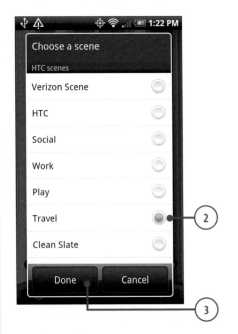

**The Home screen with
the new scene applied**

Creating Your Own Scene

You can place your own widgets, programs, and shortcuts on the Home
screen, move existing ones around,
and change the wallpaper already;
but what if you want to save what
you have done to reuse later? Well,
you can just save your creation as a
new scene.

1. Arrange the Home screens the
   way you want them by adding,
   removing, or deleting widgets
   and changing the wallpaper.
   Refer to the relevant sections in
   this chapter.

2. After you have everything laid out
   to your satisfaction on each of the
   Home screens, touch Menu and
   touch Scenes.

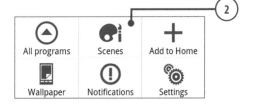

3. Make sure that Current (Unsaved) is selected.

4. Touch Save.

5. Type a name for your scene.

6. Touch Done.

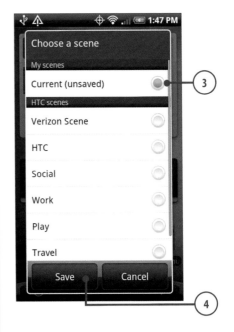

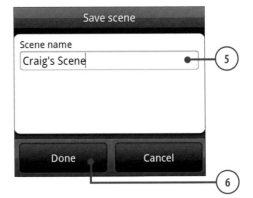

Changing Your Keyboard

If you find it hard to type on the standard Droid keyboard, or you just want to make it look better, you can install replacement keyboards. You can purchase or download replacement keyboards from the Android Market.

1. Launch Android Market and search for, purchase, or download a free keyboard replacement application. We chose one called Better Keyboard.

2. Touch the Menu button and touch Settings.

3. Touch Language & Keyboard.

Do Your Research

When you choose a different keyboard in step 4, the Droid gives you a warning telling you that nonstandard keyboards have the potential for capturing everything you type. Do your research on any keyboards before you download and install them.

4. Touch the name of a keyboard (Better Keyboard, in this case) to choose your new keyboard.

5. After you select your new keyboard, touch the Settings option for your chosen keyboard to make changes to the default settings of that keyboard. Many replacement keyboards have extra skins that change the way they look and the colors they use.

6. After you are satisfied with the settings, touch the Back button until you reach the Home screen. Your new keyboard is now used in place of the default Android keyboard.

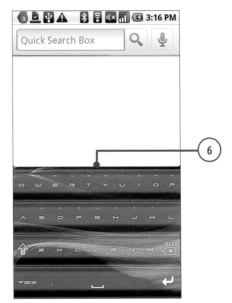

Swype Keyboard

The Swype keyboard is a revolution-
ary keyboard that enables you to
swipe your finger over the keyboard
to type as opposed to touching each
key individually. Theoretically, this
enables you to type more quickly. It's
cool whether it speeds your typing.
The Swype keyboard is preinstalled
on the Droid X. Unfortunately, it cannot be downloaded from the
Android Market. Here is how to
switch to the Swype keyboard on the
Droid X.

1. Touch the Menu button and
   touch Settings.

2. Touch Language & Keyboard.

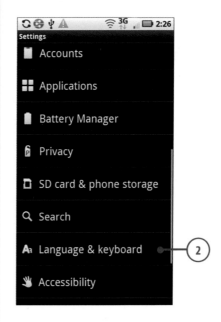

3. Touch Input Method.

4. Touch Swype.

BASICS OF SWYPE

There is a full tutorial on how to use Swype on the Droid X, but to get you going, here are the basics.

- Type a word by swiping your finger across all the keys that make up the word and then lift your finger.

- To type a double letter, circle the letter.

- To type an uppercase letter, swipe off the keyboard after swiping over the letter, then swipe over the remaining letters in the word.

- Sometimes you type a word that is too similar to another word. At that point, the Swype keyboard displays a choice of possibilities. Touch the word you want.

Adding Widgets to Your Home Screens

Some applications that you install come with widgets that can be placed on your Home screens. These widgets normally display real-time information such as stocks, weather, time, and Facebook feeds. Here is how to add and manage widgets.

Adding a Widget

Your Droid should come preinstalled with some widgets, but you might also have some extra ones that have been added when you installed other applications. Here is how to add those widgets to your Home screens.

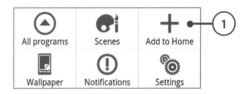

1. Touch the Menu button and touch Add to Home. Depending on the Droid, this may just say Add.

2. Touch Widgets.

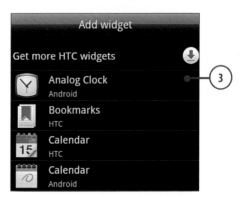

Moto Widgets

Because Android is so customizable, this screen might look different. For example, if you have a Droid X, the screen shows Motorola Widgets and Android Widgets. The Motorola Widgets are specific to Motorola Droids.

3. Touch the widget you want to add.

HTC Widgets

If you have an HTC Droid, on the Widgets screen you see a Get More HTC Widgets option. Touch this to see a list of HTC-specific widgets that you can download and use on your Droid.

5. The widget is added to the Home screen.

The newly added widget

Moving a Widget

Sometimes you want to reposition your widgets or move them to other screens. Here is how.

1. Touch and hold the widget you want to move.

2. Move your finger around the screen. As you move, a green box follows to indicate where you can move the widget to.

3. The dark regions on the screen indicate areas that are too small to accommodate the widget.

4. You can also drag the widget off the screen to the left or right to place it on an adjacent screen.

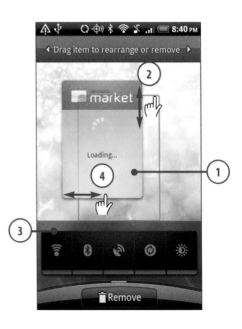

Removing a Widget

You may become tired of a certain widget or need to make space for a new widget. Here is how to remove widgets from your Home screen.

1. Touch and hold the widget you want to remove.

2. Drag the widget to the word Remove. Depending on the model of Droid, you might see a Trash icon instead of the word Remove.

3. The widget is removed from the screen, but it's still on your Droid for future use.

Region and Language

If you move to another country or want to change the language used by your Droid, you can do so with a few touches.

1. From the Home screen, touch the Menu button and touch Settings.

2. Touch Language & Keyboard.

3. Touch Select Locale.

4. Touch the language you want to switch to.

5. Your Droid instantly switches to using this new language.

Who Obeys the Language?

When you switch your Droid to use a different language, you immediately notice that all standard applications and the Droid menus switch to the new language. Even some third-party applications honor the language switch. However many third-party applications ignore the language setting on the Droid. So you might open a third-party application and find that all of its menus are still in English.

Accessibility Apps

Not all Droids include vibration, sound, and speaking apps. If your Droid doesn't, you can find these accessibility apps in the Android Market. Read more on how to use the Android Market in Chapter 10.

Screen information is now displayed in the new language

Accessibility Settings

The Droid includes built-in settings to assist people who might otherwise have difficulty using some features of the device. The Droid has the capability to provide alternative feedback such as vibration, sound, and even speaking of menus. If you have limited or no vision, these accessibility options may help.

1. While on the Home screen, touch the Menu button and then touch Settings.

2. Scroll down and touch Accessibility.

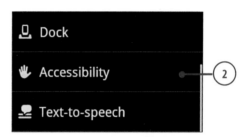

3. Touch Accessibility to enable the accessibility services. The green check mark indicates the services are turned on.

4. Touch to enable SoundBack, which plays sounds as you navigate your Droid. SoundBack adds audible queues as you navigate menus on your Droid. For example if you touch the search area, you hear a ping sound.

5. Touch to enable KickBack, which makes your Droid vibrate as you navigate menus and press buttons.

6. Touch to enable TalkBack that speaks menus, labels, and names as you navigate on your Droid.

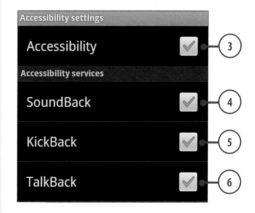

Control Volume of SoundBack and TalkBack

You can control the volume of SoundBack and TalkBack because they fall under the category of Media playback. However it is impossible to control the volume with just SoundBack enabled because the audible queues are too quick. A good trick is to enable TalkBack and, while it is reading something, adjust the volume by using the physical volume keys on the side of your Droid. After you have the desired volume, you can disable TalkBack.

Search Settings

When you search from the Home screen on your Droid, you are searching the Internet as well as content on your phone such as your contacts and browser bookmarks. You can control what to search, and you can even add YouTube as a default area to be searched.

1. While on the Home screen, touch the Menu button and then touch Settings.

2. Scroll down and touch Search.

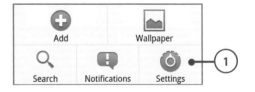

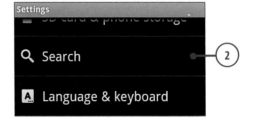

3. Touch to clear your previous search terms.

4. Touch Searchable Items to select what to search.

5. Select or deselect the content you want to be searched when you type in search terms.

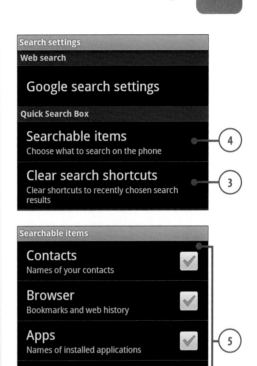

In this chapter, you learn how to maintain your Droid and solve problems. Topics include the following:

→ Updating Android
→ Obtaining battery optimization
→ Finding battery-hungry applications
→ Caring for your Droid

Maintaining Droid and Solving Problems

Every so often Google releases new versions of Android that have bug fixes and new features. In this chapter we teach you how to upgrade your Droid to a new version of Android, and we tackle common problem-solving issues and general maintenance of your Droid.

Update Information

Updates to Android are on no set schedule. Complicating matters is that there are different phones running Android, so your friend who has a different Android phone might get an update before you see the update message on your Droid. The update messages appear as you turn on your Droid, and they remain in the notification bar until you install the update. If you touch Install Later, your Droid reminds you that there's an update every 30 minutes. Sometimes people like to wait to see if any bugs need to be worked out before they update; it is up to you.

Updating Android

New releases of Android are always exciting because they add new features, fix bugs, and tweak the user interface. Here is how to update your Droid.

1. If you receive a notification that there is a system update, touch Install Now.

Manually Check for Updates

If you think there should be an update for your Droid, but have not yet received the onscreen notification, you can check manually by touching Menu, Settings, About Phone, and System Updates. If there are updates, they are listed on this screen.

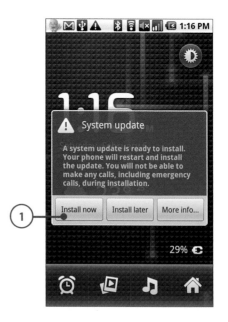

2. Touch Restart & Install. Your Droid updates and reboots.

Battery Optimizing

The battery in your Droid is a lithium ion battery that provides good battery life when you take care of it. Changing the way you use your Droid helps prolong the battery's life, which gives you more hours in a day to use your phone.

Looking After the Battery

There are specific steps you can take to correctly care for the battery in your Droid. Caring for your battery enables it to last longer.

Steps to care for your Droid's battery:

1. Try to avoid discharging the battery completely. Fully discharging the battery too frequently harms the battery. Instead, try to keep it partially charged at all

times (except as described in the next step).

2. To avoid a false battery level indication on your Droid, let the battery fully discharge about every 30 charges. Lithium-ion batteries do not have "memory" like older battery technologies; however, the battery meter is the problem.

3. Do not leave your Droid in a hot car or out in the sun anywhere, including on the beach, as this can damage the battery and make it lose its charge quickly.

4. Consider having multiple chargers. For example, you could have one at home, one at work, and maybe one at a client's site. This enables you to always keep your Droid charged.

Extending Battery Life

In addition to the tips mentioned in the preceding section, here are some things you can do while using your Droid to help prolong battery life.

1. Install a task-killer application. When you close an application, it keeps running in the background. If you aren't going to use it again that day, use the task-killer application to kill it. The more applications running, the faster you burn through the battery life.

Use a task-killer application to close apps you aren't using

Where to Find Task Killers

If you use the Android Market application, you can search for "task killer" or "task manager" and you will see hundreds of them. You don't need to pay money for one because there are many free task killers or task managers. See Chapter 10, "Working with Android Applications," for more information on how to use the Android Market.

Touch to enable or disable a radio

2. Turn off radios that you are not using. For example, if you are not using a Bluetooth headset, turn off the Bluetooth radio. Use the widget Home screen to do this quickly.

3. If you can, dim the screen and shorten the screen timeout.

4. If you don't need your email in real-time, set your Droid to synchronize manually or less frequently.

5. Touch the Menu button while on the Home screen and touch Settings.

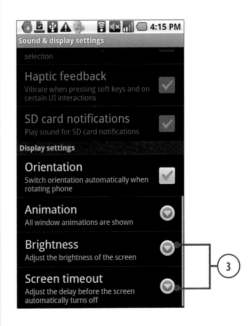

6. Touch Accounts & Sync.

7. Touch Background Data to enable or disable background synchronization. The check mark is gray when you have this disabled, and you no longer receive email in real-time. Calendar and contacts do not update in real-time either.

8. Touch Auto-sync to enable or disable automatic data synchronization. If you disable this, changes you make to contacts and calendar are not automatically synchronized to the online contacts and calendar. When background synchronization is disabled, you can manually synchronize your contacts and calendar.

9. From the Accounts & Sync Settings screen, touch an account.

10. Touch a specific data set to synchronize it manually.

11. Touch the Menu button and
touch Sync Now to synchronize all
data sets on the screen.

See What Is Using Power

Your Droid has a feature that tells
you what applications are using the
most power. You can use this feature
to adjust how you use your phone to
help extend battery life.

1. Touch the Menu button and
touch Settings.

2. Touch About Phone.

3. Touch Battery Use. You see a list of applications and what percentage of time they used the battery since the last charge.

4. Touch an application to see more information.

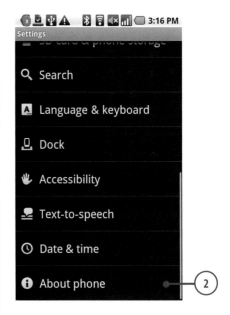

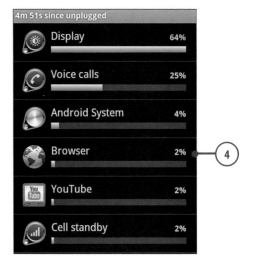

5. Depending on the application, you see extra information including how much data it sent and received.

Number of seconds of CPU time this application has used while in the foreground

Number of seconds of CPU time this application has used in total

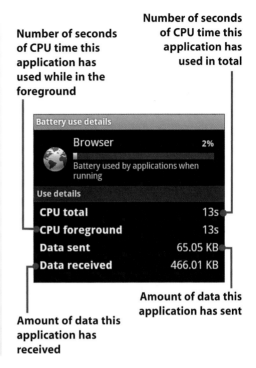

Amount of data this application has sent

Amount of data this application has received

Dealing with Misbehaving Applications

Sometimes applications misbehave and slow down your Droid. You can use a task-killer application as we discussed in the "Extending Battery Life" section, or you can use the Droid's built-in feature to forcefully close an application.

1. Touch the Menu button and touch Settings.

2. Touch Applications.

3. Touch Manage Applications.

When to Force Quit an Application

After you have been using your Droid for a while, you'll become familiar with how long it takes to do certain tasks such as typing, navigating menus, and so on. If you notice your Droid becoming slow or not behaving the way you remember it, the culprit could be a new application you recently installed. Because Android never quits applications on its own, that new application continues running in the background and causing your Droid to slow down. This is when it is useful to use force quit.

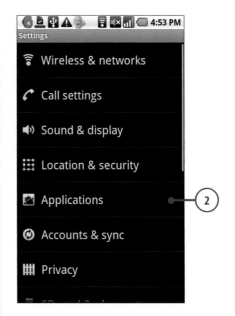

4. Touch the Menu button and touch Filter.

5. Touch Running to filter the display to show only applications that are currently running.

6. Touch the misbehaving application.

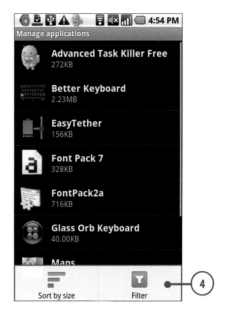

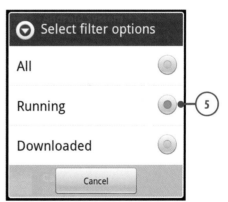

7. Touch Force Stop. The screen does not update, but the application stops running. If you go back to the list of applications, you see that the application is no longer visible.

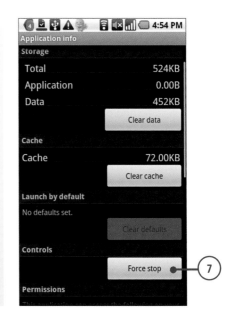

Caring for Droid's Exterior

Because you need to touch your Droid's screen to use it, it picks up oils and other residue from your hands. You also might get dirt on other parts of the phone. Here is how to clean your Droid.

1. Wipe the screen with a microfiber cloth. You can purchase these in most electronic stores, or you can use the one that came with your sunglasses.

2. To clean dirt off other parts of your phone, wipe it with a damp cloth. Never use soap or chemicals on your Droid as they can damage it.

3. When inserting the Micro-USB connector, try not to force it in the wrong way. If you damage the pins inside your Droid, you cannot charge it unless you have the dock.

Getting Help with Your Droid

There are many resources on the Internet where you can get help with your Droid.

1. Visit the Official Google website at http://www.android.com.

2. Check out some Android blogs:

    • Android Central at http://www.androidcentral.com/

    • Android Guys at http://www.androidguys.com/

    • Androinica at http://androinica.com/

3. Contact me. I don't mind answering your questions, so visit my official My Droid site at http://www.CraigsBooks.info.

Index

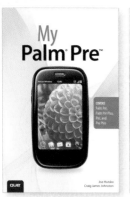

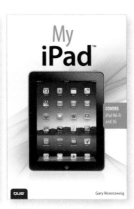

DEC 0 1 2010

My Droid™

Covers
Droid Incredible,
Droid Eris, Droid X,
Droid 1 & 2

que®   Craig James Johnston

FREE Online Edition

Your purchase of **My Droid™** includes access to a free online edition for 45 days through the Safari Books Online subscription service. Nearly every Que book is available online through Safari Books Online, along with more than 5,000 other technical books and videos from publishers such as Addison-Wesley Professional, Cisco Press, Exam Cram, IBM Press, O'Reilly, Prentice Hall, and Sams.

SAFARI BOOKS ONLINE allows you to search for a specific answer, cut and paste code, download chapters, and stay current with emerging technologies.

Activate your FREE Online Edition at
www.informit.com/safarifree

> **STEP 1:** Enter the coupon code: NRXSPVH.

> **STEP 2:** New Safari users, complete the brief registration form.
> Safari subscribers, just log in.

If you have difficulty registering on Safari or accessing the online edition, please e-mail customer-service@safaribooksonline.com